Sea Questions

Identity, origins and adoption

Julia Feast and Terry Philpot

BAAF
ADOPTION
& FOSTERING

Published by
British Association for Adoption & Fostering
(BAAF)
Skyline House
200 Union Street
London SE1 0LX
www.baaf.org.uk

Charity registration 275689

© Julia Feast and Terry Philpot, 2003

British Library Cataloguing in Publication Data
A catalogue record for this book is available from the British Library

ISBN 1 903699 47 9

Project management by Shaila Shah, Director of Publications, BAAF
Photographs on cover posed by models by John Birdsall Photography
www.johnbirdsall.co.uk
Designed by Andrew Haig & Associates
Typeset by Jonathan Harley
Printed by The Russell Press (TU) Nottingham

Contents

Acknowledgements

Many people have helped us to produce *Searching Questions*. Firstly, we would like to thank all the adopted people who feature in the video and are quoted in this workbook, as well as those others whose stories were first told in *Adoption, Search and Reunion*. Without them, this enterprise would not have been possible. Their stories have been illuminating and inspirational.

This workbook draws on the research reported in *Adoption, Search and Reunion*; we thank Professor David Howe, the principal author of that study, for permission to draw upon its findings and also for his valuable contribution to scoping this project in its initial stages.

This workbook and the video that accompanies it were first conceived of when Julia Feast was working at The Children's Society. We must thank, in particular, those people from the Post Adoption and Care Counselling Project at The Children's Society's office in Peckham, London, who contributed to initial discussions about the project. They include: Rose Wallace, Janet Smith, Jenny Setterington, Casia Davies, Gayle Martin, Tricia Scott, Erica Peltier, Penny Whittingham; Elizabeth Webb previously at the Children's Society and now at The Adolescent and Children Trust (TACT) and Julia Pearmain from BAAF. They were our original reference group whose advice and suggestions have been enormously helpful.

The video that accompanies this book was filmed by Mark Slocombe of CreationVideos; thanks are due to Sue Hyam for transcribing the filmed interviews, to Danielle Sawyer for typing parts of this script and to Jo Francis for her help with checking proofs.

We would particularly like to thank Fran Moffat, Trainer Consultant at BAAF Southern Region, for her help with developing the questions and exercises; Elizabeth Webb, from TACT, and John Simmonds, Director of Policy, Research and Development at BAAF, for their comments and suggestions which have been critical to the final product; and Shaila Shah, Director of Publications at BAAF, for managing the project and taking it through to publication.

Finally, this project would not have been realised without the very generous funding given by The Nuffield Foundation, which supported this project over a six-year period to enable The Children's Society, and now BAAF, to undertake research in this important area and to publish this resource. Particular thanks must extend to Sharon Witherspoon, Deputy Director of The Nuffield Foundation, for the unstinting support she has given us and the guidance she has offered.

Julia Feast and Terry Philpot, October 2003

→

Notes about the authors

Julia Feast is the Policy, Research & Development Consultant at BAAF. In the past she has managed The Children's Society's Post Adoption & Care: Counselling & Research Project, worked as a local authority social worker and Team Manager and also as a Guardian ad litem and Reporting Officer. She has published many articles on the subject of adoption, search and reunion and also on the information needs of children conceived as a result of donor-assisted conception. She is co-author of *Preparing for Reunion: Experiences from the adoption circle* (The Children's Society 1994, new edition 1998) and *Adoption, Search and Reunion: The long-term experience of adopted adults* (The Children's Society 2000; republished by BAAF 2003). She is a member of the Department for Education and Skills' Adoption and Permanency Taskforce.

Terry Philpot is a writer on social policy and was formerly Editor and Editor in Chief of *Community Care*. He has written and edited several books, including *Action for Children*; *Values and Visions: Changing ideas in services for people with learning difficulties* (with Linda Ward); *Sweet Charity: The work and role of voluntary organisations* (with Chris Hanvey); *Caring and Coping: A guide to social services* (with Anthony Douglas); *Political Correctness and Social Work* and *A Very Private Practice*. His latest book, *Adoption: Changing lives, changing times* (with Anthony Douglas) was published by Routledge in 2002. He is a trustee of the Social Care Institute for Excellence and of the Centre for Policy on Ageing and RPS-Rainer and a member of the advisory committee for the Economic and Social Research Council's Growing Older Programme. He has won several awards for journalism.

foreword

How to use this Workbook

Searching Questions is a resource consisting of this workbook and an accompanying video; although the book and video complement each other, they are not interdependent. They have been produced with a range of readers and viewers in mind.

☐ Social workers and other professionals with an interest in different aspects of adoption will find them useful in group work with birth parents, adoptive parents, and the adopted child or young person. This resource lends itself to being used by a trainer who can facilitate the group work – the questions at the end of each section will stimulate discussion and the exercises and the video can be flexibly used in a group setting.

☐ People directly involved in adoption – birth parents, adoptive parents and adopted people themselves – will find much that is helpful. For those considering adopting a child, it will alert them to an adopted person's desire to search for their origins and learn about their identity. For birth parents who have parted with a child for adoption, it will remind them of the part that they continue to play in their now adopted child's life; the significance of information about family history and origins; and that being contacted could be a very real possibility. For adopted people themselves, it offers much food for thought about searching, the journey, and the challenges that could face them – all this illuminated by the real life examples of those who have chosen, or not, to do so.

☐ Those teaching basic and advanced social work courses will find the material helpful across a range of topics – child and human development, separation and loss, family placement, adoption and identity, and the implications for all concerned.

☐ Anybody concerned with, or interested in, the passion that can drive people to undertake long and complicated journeys to find out more about where they came from, who they were and who they are will also find this book of great interest.

☐ Infertility counsellors, those born as a result of donor-assisted conception, donors themselves and the parents of such children will also gain insights about the identity needs of donor-conceived children.

The book is divided into short chapters, each of which explores particular areas and is illustrated with quotations from people and ends with questions that prompt further exploration, as well as exercises that can be used in group work. The video, which is

→

available from BAAF, presents the experiences of searchers and non-searchers, as told by adopted people themselves.

This resource will be fascinating for anyone wanting to explore further the complexity of the human spirit and human relationships. All the stories told here have the power of drama, but there is a difference – these stories are true.

introduction

Most people, adopted or not, often wonder about the small change of existence – Where does my tone of voice come from? Why do I have a special aptitude for music? If my child looks like me, is that a trait that runs in the family? Why was my father mild when my grandmother was argumentative? For those of us who are not adopted, such questions can often be answered by enquiring of our own parents, grandparents, aunts and uncles or older brothers and sisters. We can also spot family likenesses in our nieces and nephews, cousins, and grandchildren and grandparents.

Many adopted people ask the same questions but when they do, they do so as part of a larger quest – to search for their birth family to seek what many people call "completeness" and to establish a sense of identity.

Adopted people's search and reunion with birth parents is beginning to be more widely reported. It has been the subject of television coverage, as well as research studies and articles in the professional press. The results of this, especially when such reunions work out well, have a deep resonance with us as human beings. Memories, expectations, hope, and disappointment all come into play and affect not just the searcher but everyone in the adoption circle – adopted person, adoptive family and birth family, as well as partners and children. Each, however, may experience the process very differently.

And yet the wish to search and find birth relatives is not something that affects all adopted people. There are those who do not seek information about their origins, who do not want to meet family members, and whose level of genealogical interest is very low and sometimes even non-existent. Why this should be so is as interesting as why others choose to search. Choosing not to make that journey has its own implications for others, just as does the decision to do so.

While these and other matters affect all of us as human beings, there are also others which are filtered through our "race", our sense of heritage, our culture and our customs. The experiences of those adopted by strangers may be different to those who are adopted by family (which would include the partner of a parent). Those who were adopted as babies or very small children will be different to those who came to their adoptive families when they were older.

Adoption is not a small, discrete part of social work practice. Nearly 900,000 people have been adopted since adoption became legal in England and Wales in 1926 (in Scotland in 1930 and in Northern Ireland in 1950). Between 1975 and 1997, there were 74,000 applications for birth records counselling in England and Wales. But →

even this does not tell the whole story – the number of people touched by adoption is thought to be one in four in the UK.

The Children Act 1975 (and subsequently, the Adoption Act 1976) made it possible for adopted people in England and Wales to apply for a copy of their original birth certificate if they wished and by so doing opened opportunities for them to search for birth relatives. In Scotland, adopted people over the age of 21 could do so since 1930 and in Northern Ireland since 1987.

With the right of adopted people to information about their origins has come the chance for adoption practitioners, managers and policy makers to learn much more about what it means to be adopted and to be separated from one's roots, birth family and heritage. For example, although adopted people may not always speak about it, they do think about their birth families when growing up. For many birth relatives – mainly birth mothers – the making of the adoption order does not mean that thoughts of their child are banished from their mind. For many – adopted person and birth parent – feelings of concern and curiosity, sadness or loss continue over the years.

Adoption practice today involves a far higher degree of openness so that thoughts like 'What is my birth mother like?' 'Do I have birth brothers and sisters?' 'Do I have a grandparent alive?' can often be answered. Adoptive parents are given much fuller details about their child's birth family and background. Adopted children are usually given a life story book, which will include details of family members and photographs. This means that questions about family likeness and other genealogical details can be answered much more directly.

But adoption is far more than a paper exercise. It involves real people, often living very different lives; people with emotions, knowledge, fears and hopes. The search for the birth parent – or the decision not to search – involves a move into very sensitive, very personal and very emotive territory.

For the adopted person who decides to search, a "successful" search may not mean that there is a happy conclusion – the parent may have refused to meet the adopted person or if they had a meeting it may have been a brief one. But there are many more instances where the search has satisfied both the adopted person and birth parent – it may not have been the start of a new relationship (though it certainly can be) and may be no more than that the parent learned that their child was happy and healthy and the child had their curiosity satisfied. That may be enough.

People are very often interested in why some adopted people search and why others do not. The reasons behind this are complex. Some people believe that to search means that an adopted person who searches must be unhappy about their adoption but research has shown that, in fact, 53 per cent of searchers described their adoption as positive and happy.

Search and reunion in adoption have a wider relevance than just adoption. At its root it is about separation from one's birth parents, even if one never knew them. Adopted people live in families and circumstances, which, had things been different, they would never have known or experienced. That is why there may be more general lessons about how people react to separation, for example, children who are taken into public care or are born as a result of donor-assisted conception.

The experience of wartime evacuation helped society to think about the impact on children separated from their families and living with other families, often for long periods of time, in very different environments to those in which they had grown up – for example, the child from inner-city London placed in rural Norfolk. So today, knowledge about adopted people's experiences of their birth and adoptive families, their lives and the reasons why they search or not, may help us to understand the issues for other children when they become adults, for example, children seeking asylum in the UK.

Adoption also throws into sharp relief those age-old issues of nature and nurture. Adopted people who trace and get to know their birth families may be well placed to answer, from their personal experiences, some of these questions.

In 2000, more than 25 years since the legislative change which gave adopted people the right to have access to the information held on their birth certificate, a major research study was published by The Children's Society: *Adoption, Search and Reunion: The long-term experience of adopted adults* by David Howe and Julia Feast.* The study involved nearly 500 adopted people. While there have been previous studies about adopted people, this research was the first to look at why some adopted people choose to seek their birth families and others do not. The authors compared 394 adult adopted people who searched ("searchers") with 78 adopted people who chose not to do so ("non-searchers"). Thirty-three of the adopted adults had been placed in a transracial placement. The study examined why adopted people search for information about their background ("searchers") and contrasts their experiences with adopted people who have shown no apparent interest in accessing information from adoption records or searching for birth relatives ("non-searchers"). The study also looked at the long-term nature of adopted people's restored relationship with their birth relatives and their continuing relationship with the adoptive family.

This workbook is based on that study and readers should assume that findings are taken from it unless otherwise stated. It should be noted that the parts of chapters entitled "What research tells us" make use of research from Howe and Feast and not from other studies. This is because, first, this workbook is based on the Howe and Feast study but, second, that, as has been said, that study is the first of its kind. Other research concerned with some of the areas focused on in *Adoption, Search and Reunion* complements these findings. The workbook also draws on the presentations given by adopted people at a conference in London about search and reunion, held on 23 March 2000, and other interviews with adopted people who have either taken the decision to search or not to search for birth relatives. All of these will be found on the accompanying video.

Adoption, Search and Reunion was republished by BAAF in November 2003. The title, authors and text remain the same with an updated introduction.

→

With three exceptions (Anna, Jane and Sandy) these testimonies come from people who were adopted through The Children's Society. These quotations have been supplemented by others taken from *Adoption, Search and Reunion (A, S&R)* and where quotations are taken from that source they are followed by (*A, S&R*). The full quotations are used to illustrate the range of experiences and issues that face adopted people, and those facing their birth and adoptive families. Some quotations may be repeated in different sections in the book as the content may be relevant to different issues and experiences. The workbook, like the *Adoption, Search and Reunion* study, uses pseudonyms. The real names of the people who feature in the video are given. However, as two of the video interviewees, Heather and David, have the same names as two of the pseudonyms used in the book, we have left their names as they are. They can be distinguished by the fact that Heather and David from the book are identified, as we state above, by the source appearing after extracts from their testimonies.

The workbook should, therefore, be used in conjunction with the video that records the stories of those who have searched and those who have chosen not to (and in one case, of a person who is a foundling, and therefore is unable to do so).

This resource, that is the workbook and video, can be used together for a range of audiences to highlight issues involved in search and reunion and to provide a greater understanding of the complexities and feelings that may be encountered on the way. For example, they can be used to help prepare prospective adoptive parents about the needs of adopted children; to prepare adopted adults about what may happen when deciding to search and seek reunion; or to help birth parents to understand the emotions which come to adopted people. They will also prove useful when used in other areas where identity, family relationships, and separation and loss are of concern. These may be as various as intercountry adoption, the preparation of the prospective parents of a child to be conceived by donor assistance, or children who have been privately fostered – the last will very often be black but placed with white families in all-white communities.

This resource can also be used as part of a training course, or less formally. It can be used by groups or by just two or three people, or even one person on their own.

Inevitably, the people who feature in the video and whose lives are reflected in these pages are old enough to have been able to make use of their right to search under the 1975 legislation – some are themselves parents, the youngest is in her 30s. Since they were adopted much has changed: for example, fewer children are placed for adoption today in the UK, but an increasing number are being adopted from overseas, about 300 per year, and there is much more openness in adoption and, with the Adoption and Children Act 2002, this will be greater still. However, many of the issues which surround adoption remain because adoption is about human beings relating to each other, rejection and acceptance, anxiety and resolution, hope and disappointment, attachment and loss, and having a sense of identity. Thus it is that while adopted adults continue to seek help in searching for their birth relatives, many of the issues which are raised here are ones which will face even the newly adopted, different though their experience will have been, when they reach 18 and have the opportunity to search. But even before then, much of what is reported and discussed here will have a resonance and practical use for people adopting now and for those children whom they adopt.

Helping people through the various stages of search and possible reunion is not only a socially valuable process but also a very humanly sensitive and emotionally demanding one. It can mean dealing with heart-breaking disappointment, as well as sharing in real joy. This means that it is work that requires a high degree of professionalism, as well as compassion and commitment.

This resource aims to take users step by step through all that is involved. Questions and exercises are provided at the end of each chapter of this workbook. These are intended to help stimulate discussion for those working in groups, as well as to assist reflection and provoke thought by those who use the workbook on their own.

Thus, it is intended that, illustrated by the words of searchers and non-searchers alike, this workbook will help practitioners to help others on a journey where truth is often more involving than fiction and the final destination may be unpredictable.

1

A child in the family: growing up adopted

A CHILD IN THE FAMILY

Introduction

Childhood memories and experiences inevitably shape who we are and what we become as adults. In turn this impacts on the way we make relationships and the meaning these have in our lives. Growing up as an adopted child will mean that there are additional issues to deal with. For some children their adoptive status will be openly discussed and they may have a good understanding of why they were placed for adoption and other information about their original family background. For others, it may be an uncomfortable subject that is rarely referred to. For a few, there may be a seal of silence and an unspoken agreement that adoption and the information that relates to the birth family is not spoken about at all. In whatever way families manage these complex issues and however they are woven into the fabric of their relationships, the facts and the fantasies about being adopted will form a powerful context for individual development.

Most families have secrets. Although some "secrets" are harmless, for example, not telling someone about a nice surprise they are about to have, others can have a potentially harmful effect. The need to maintain a secret is not usually something that is done out of malice but often out of a need to protect the person the secret is about. It is often justified as being necessary to protect the person from information that may be shameful, upsetting or hurtful, for example, the death or disappearance of a family member in difficult circumstances, a family rift because of a fight over inheritance, the birth of a child after an extra-marital affair or incest, a physical impairment following an accident after a drunken night out. Most secrets revolve around sex or money or both and there is little that is as potent in creating secrets as these two ingredients. People fear the consequences if the secret is disclosed as it can have a major impact on family relationships and dynamics.

But maintaining a secret has its own consequences. In particular, it keeps the subject of the secret alive in an unhelpful and potentially dangerous way and means that it cannot be resolved. Where it involves constructing alternative stories and explanations, these can have a life of their own that generate their own anxiety and fear.

Where the secret revolves around adoption or a child's adoptive status, the impact can be as great as any other secret. For those involved, it will impact on family structure, relationships and communication as well as preventing the person concerned from making informed decisions about their lives. Take the case of the woman whose adoptive status was told to her for the first time at a family funeral when she was 50 years old. She was married but had made the painful decision not to have any children, as her brother had died of a genetically inherited disease and she did not want this passed on to any of her offspring. The very late realisation that she had been adopted, and that she had no genetic link to her brother, had enormous consequences for her that could have been avoided if she had been told the truth about her origins.

The reasons behind the secret may be based on good intentions but it may mean that the act of deceit will hurt the adopted person more. Maintaining a secret can also have profound implications for the person who holds it. Relationships may be put under strain and people may be constantly worried about disclosure of the secret or feel guilty that they are not being open and honest.

What research tells us

The majority of adults interviewed in *Adoption Search and Reunion* knew that they were adopted. In fact, most people said that it was something they could not recall being told, it was just something they always knew. Over 68 per cent of "searchers" and "non-searchers" said that they had been told under the age of five.

But even though most adopted people knew that they were adopted, talking about adoption or their background was not easy. Less than 30 per cent of both searchers and non-searchers in the study felt comfortable talking to their adoptive parents about their adoption and birth family. For 35 per cent of searchers and 26 per cent of non-searchers, their adoptive parents never discussed the background to the adoption. On the other hand, 16 per cent of searchers and 12 per cent of non-searchers said that their parents had given them a lot of information about the background to their adoption.

Whether information was given or not, most adopted people had thought particularly about their birth mother or other birth relatives while growing up. Over 80 per cent of searchers and non-searchers had wondered what their birth parent looked like and whether they had any physical characteristics in common. Some people thought about their birth parents a lot while growing up while others did not do so until they were teenagers.

The vast majority of adopted people felt loved by their adoptive parents while they were growing up. Sixty-eight per cent of searchers and 85 per cent of non-searchers said that they felt they belonged to their adoptive parents. But it is clear that "feeling loved" and a "sense of belonging" to one's adoptive parents does not stop people feeling different; 50 per cent of searchers and 27 per cent of non-searchers described feeling "different". Sometimes the sense of difference was marked by the lack of physical similarity. This was exacerbated in situations where children had been placed in a transracial placement or where black or children of mixed heritage were placed in a white family. But feeling different may not just be because of physical difference but also due to different personality traits and interests. For example, an adopted person who may be hopeless at sport but particularly talented at music may have been adopted by a family who have no particular interest in music, but have a great passion for sporting activities.

→

Openness and communication

One of the most difficult tasks for adoptive parents reported in *Adoption, Search and Reunion* is being able to talk openly to their son or daughter about their adoption. It may be that they do not want to raise the subject if the child has not expressed any interest but it may also be because the child, whether consciously or subconsciously, feels uncomfortable too. Talking about or expressing an interest in their birth family may seem disloyal or imply a criticism of adoptive parents as not being good enough. As Angela said:

> *Adoption was not talked about at all. I sensed my parents just didn't want to talk about it at all. They were just being protective towards me and ... any questions that I asked they weren't always talked about. If I asked they would say, 'well you don't need to know about that' or they didn't know. (A, S&R, p. 80)*

It does seem to make it much easier for adopted people if they have always known the fact of their adoption status and if the subject can be discussed openly, without it feeling that the subject is taboo. According to Helen:

> *I've always known, as early as I can remember. My parents were open insofar as they told us [and her brother who was also adopted] and they had a little story book about how children were adopted, how special we were that we were adopted. (A, S&R, p. 76)*

Anna says the same:

> *I don't remember being told I was adopted, but apparently this happened when I was five or six years old – it must have been handled very sensitively because I certainly never remember it being a problem or an issue to me. I knew I was part of the family, most of my friends seemed to know as well – I think my parents must have told most of my friends' parents – so it was very much in the open and not a secret.*

Andrew, too, had a similar experience:

> *My adoptive parents were always very honest with me when discussing my origins – I am unaware of a time when I didn't know that I was adopted and I can still remember them reading* Mr and Mrs Fairweather *to me. Much to their credit, they even told me that my birth mother had tried to keep me and that I was really wanted.*

And so did Carol, who attests to openness:

> *As a small child my parents made me aware I was adopted and told me a little information. I think it was that old chestnut that I'd been chosen whereas in most families their children just arrived and they had no say in the matter – they had particularly chosen me. Then*

> *there were more details given, I think – again, there's no particular moment at which I found information out but I did know ... the limited information I have ... I think I've always sort of known or asked again to be reminded.*

Carol tells the story of how her mother used to raise funds for The Children's Society by going out collecting the collection boxes. Carol, then still a small child, used to go with her and her mother's easy attitude with her about her adoption was apparent in the joke she would make that when she married Carol's father she had paid for him once when she had to buy the marriage licence but she had to pay for Carol every year by sending the money off!

Sandy is a foundling but her family was also open about her having been adopted:

> *I always knew I was adopted – my older sister was adopted – and it was quite an open subject within the family. My younger sister was natural but that didn't seem to make any difference at all – we were all aware of our beginnings ...*

There is, however, a fine balance between discussing adoption and the child's background openly so that they feel comfortable and raising the subject in a way that reminds the child of their different status. As David said:

> *I've always known that I was adopted – I've always grown up with that knowledge. My parents never consciously ever sat me down at a certain time in my life and said: 'Look here, we've got this to tell you – you're adopted.' It was always made known to me – as soon as I could comprehend things – so I've always been used to that knowledge ... And when I was young it was never an issue with me because I always looked on mum and dad as the people who raised me – although I always knew that I did not originally come from them ...*
>
> > *Discussion of adoption was never taboo in the family – all knew that we were adopted [three of his five brothers and sisters were adopted]. They were all treated the same as me and certainly between the four of us it was never a problem. There was no contest over it. We all knew we were adopted and it never really figured between us; it was never discussed that much.*

Anna's experience shows how knowing that she was adopted did not mean that she did not feel at one with her family:

> *I never felt different to my adoptive family – people even used to say I looked like them. My father, in particular, tried very hard to make sure I felt very special, that I was a "chosen one", that they had very much wanted a daughter and they were lucky enough to be able to choose me. So, generally speaking, I had a very content and happy, and what I would call stable, childhood. My parents stayed together, I had a*

→

good relationship with my older brothers, still do, and I still see my adoptive family on a very regular basis.

However, as important as openness is in creating a sense of belonging, it is also important to be able to acknowledge physical and other differences so that the child can understand why he or she does not resemble other family members or has different talents and interests. Isobel makes this point:

I'm mixed race so it's pretty obvious that I look a bit different ... we've always been brought up as a family but I am different to them in character. I was quite outgoing and did a lot of tennis when I was younger – I was quite sporty, active, lots of friends, going out trying to get to parties, whereas, for example, my older sister who's not adopted was more quiet. (A, S&R, p. 86)

Carol also refers to this:

I didn't realise I was any different to anybody else's experience in the village where I grew up. I felt no different – I had a mum and a dad like everybody else and it wasn't particularly referred to – there were enough occasions, I think, where people said 'Oh, you do look like your mother' and my mother and I grinned at each other in a sort of knowing way. But I wasn't made to feel any different. The children – my friends in the village – never even referred to it ... I didn't go around saying I was adopted but if somebody asked I would easily reply and give them enough information and then we'd go on to the next topic.

In fact, Carol describes herself as being lucky as she was adopted by parents who shared similar interests and attributes to her and this meant that, although there was not a genetic relationship between them, it made her feel very much part of the family. She says:

Growing up in an adopted family, I think, I was quite aware that I was very lucky that I was similar to, and fitted in with the family that I had. I was fortunate enough to have a father who was a teacher and quite academic and I had an interest in maths that he took and developed and pushed, in fact. So that I went to university and felt very supported by my family in going down an academic route.

Beth, however, gives an example of what it can be like to feel different to one's adopted family:

I looked different and I knew I was different. My parents are blue-eyed and I was a lot darker. There were certainly no physical resemblances. They didn't draw these to my attention. I don't remember it being mentioned. I think I was very conscious of it more than anyone else. (A, S&R, p. 86)

The extended family and the community

It is important for all children to feel that they belong and are accepted by their family and the community in which they live. But there can be particular concerns for adopted children when friends or adults find out about their different status. It can generate a lot of interest or surprise or anxiety. They may want to know what it feels like to be adopted or not to know your "real" parents. As Jane says:

> Ever since I was a little girl I never remember a time when I didn't know ... I do remember when I was at primary school age – about five or six – that I mentioned to another girl in my class that I was adopted and she found that very fascinating because I don't think that she had ever met anyone that had ever been adopted before ...

For children who are transracially adopted, there is an additional and often problematic dimension when growing up. They do not see themselves reflected in the physical characteristics of their adoptive parents and may not do so in the community in which they live. They may not see their birth family's culture or religion meaningfully reflected in their daily life. Individual and institutionalised racism may also impact significantly on them. Children who have been adopted into a family that is from a different ethnic background and culture to their own will inevitably face additional challenges in securing an identity with which they feel comfortable.

Chapter 7 of this workbook looks specifically at the experience of transracially adopted people but we refer briefly to the matter here through the experience of Estelle:

> There were only four black kids in the school John and I went to ... I just stayed in at weekends and I wouldn't go out with my friends at night. I just felt there was no point because I was too dark and things like that ... I realised when I was in my teens 'cos I knew that there had to be more to life than just coming home and crying and just doing your homework ... I did get a lot of support from my family ... I don't know whether I blamed them, because I sort of did, I think, for adopting me and bringing

lives | Andrew

Andrew was adopted in 1964 at a few months old. He began his search for his birth mother at the age of 24, and it was exceptionally quick as she had left contact details on the agency's adoption records. Since their first meeting in 1988 they have continued to have a close and fulfilling relationship. Although much effort has been made by all parties over the years to establish a relationship with birth siblings, this has not worked, and there is now no contact between them. Andrew has also met his birth father and paternal relatives but this meeting was less successful and they have not remained in touch. Andrew is the father of two children and works as an academic.

Andrew describes how his relationship with his birth mother has developed and the challenges it has brought over the years.

→

> *me into a community that was obviously quite hostile to some people.
> So I sort of blamed them and that's why I was rude to them and
> everything. But then I felt grateful that they wanted to do something
> about it, you know, by going to school – but then that just got worse.
> (A, S&R, p. 89)*

Although adoptive parents may be deeply committed and accepting of their adopted child, other family members may not accept a child into the family and treat them equally. This was Peter's experience:

> *My adoptive parents were brilliant … they loved me and treated me
> as their own all my life and I've never been anything else but their son
> … but I did feel treated unequally by my grandparents, and this hurt. I
> mean there is always that stigma at the back when you think you're
> different. My grandparents actually treated me different. My brother
> was younger than me and my parents' natural child … was actually
> spoilt more than me, although my parents did everything to
> discourage that, it was still there … my grandmother would always
> offer him things and I was sort of left out. Well it's upsetting to be
> honest with you. (A, S&R, p. 89)*

Other adopted people have said things like:

> *They didn't have any photographs of me but they did of their other
> grandchildren.*

> *I was left out of the family tree.*

> *My father's mother cut him and us out of her will.*

Craig talks about how he felt very loved by his adoptive parents but at the same time felt insecure that this love could be taken away if he caused any trouble or rocked the boat. He felt that he had been lucky to have been given a home and family and therefore felt grateful. He says:

> *Growing up adopted was … well, obviously at the time I didn't know it
> was any different to growing up as a … in a normal way … as growing
> up with your birth parents. The only lasting thing that stuck in me [was
> that] I felt that I was lucky I had a home and so there was a lasting
> thought that I owed them something for giving me a house and a home
> – but they were very loving and very caring and I got a lot of fun out of it.*

However, at the same time others felt that, no matter what they did or achieved, the love they received was unconditional.

Relationship with adoptive families

The majority of adopted people in *Adoption, Search and Reunion* felt loved and accepted by their adoptive parents. As Linda, a searcher, says:

I was very much loved, very much wanted. I was given a great deal of love, encouraged to achieve what I could, but was never pushed to do something I really couldn't do. (A, S&R, p. 94)

But, as we have said already, feeling that you are loved and happy with your adoptive family does not necessarily quench the desire to find out more about your origins. However, adopted people who make the decision to search or make contact with a birth relative often express a real desire not to hurt their adoptive parents in the process. Adopted people very often feel a great deal of concern for their adoptive parents. They do not want them to feel that the love and affection they have for them will change as a result of contact and reunion with a birth relative.

When David, a non-searcher, received a letter from the adoption agency, he was very concerned that his adoptive mother should be fully aware that his birth mother had made contact through an intermediary:

The first thing I did actually was to ring my mother to let her know – because in that short space of time I realised I wanted to do it – something inside me made me realise that I must go further with this – and I told my mother and she gave me her blessing ...

Jane, a non-searcher, also describes how concerned she felt for her adoptive parents and although she knew that they would support her if she made a decision to search, she was aware that it was likely to hurt them as well:

I think if I talked to my parents about searching I think my father, in particular, would be terribly hurt, really, really hurt. And I think my mother would be hurt but be prepared to see it perhaps from my point of view if I wanted to ... I think they would both support me – but it would be very painful for them, it would be painful for me and I've got a brother as well – who's also adopted – he's in the same situation, he's never wanted to search. And, again, he knows a little bit about his birth parents, not very much but a little bit.

Carol, another non-searcher, expresses the same sentiments:

I think she [her adoptive mother] would be surprised if not a little hurt. But I think she would also support me if I wanted to do that.

And Jane says:

I could talk to my mother about being adopted – the adoption process – but not my father. As far as he's concerned I'm his little girl and nobody else's. But with my mother I felt a lot more comfortable and she told me quite a few bits and pieces over the years.

→

Questions

☐ What is the best time to tell a child that he or she is adopted?

☐ How often should the subject of adoption be brought up?

☐ Where would you seek help if telling and being open feels uncomfortable?

☐ How do you create an atmosphere of openness?

☐ For adopters with a child in placement, what are your specific anxieties about your child's past?

☐ What do you fear the consequences will be if you are open with your child?

☐ In what special circumstances might information be kept back from the child?

☐ What are the advantages and disadvantages about being told that you are "special"?

☐ How can adoptive parents recognise the differences between themselves and their adopted child without over-emphasising them?

Exercises

Adoption professionals
Split into three small groups and discuss one of the following questions. Report back to the larger group.

Group 1: What are the fears and anxieties that work against adoptive parents being open about adoption?

Group 2: How can being open about adoption enhance the adopted person's sense of stability rather than diminish it?

Group 3: What practical help and responses need to be provided to facilitate more open and comfortable communication?

Adoptive parents and adoption professionals: small group discussion.

○ Think of the ways in which the feelings a child may have of being different from the family (in terms of looks or history) might be used in a positive way to reinforce his or her identity.

○ Think of different things adoptive parents can do to help the adopted child or young person feel comfortable talking about his or her origins and other questions relating to their adoption.

Exercises continued

○ How can the information and identity needs be addressed and met when an adopted person has a disability that prevents them expressing their own wishes and feelings?

○ How can we ensure that the group of adopted people who are foundlings have a sense of connectedness when there is no family history or even an exact date of birth?

○ How can life story books, photographs of where the child was found and historical information about other children who are also foundlings (such as Moses) help the adopted person build a greater sense of personal identity and self-worth?

Teachers and school staff

○ How can teachers and other school staff be more aware and sensitive to the particular needs of a child separated from their birth family?

○ Which areas of the curriculum will require extra sensitivity when working with an adopted child?

○ Are there any circumstances when it is appropriate for teachers to use a different approach when managing an adopted child's behaviour?

2

To search or not to search? Answering the questions "Why?" and "Why not?"

Introduction

It is important to understand why some adopted people embark on a search for their birth parents or relatives and others do not. For most people, the decision to search is not made quickly. Many adopted children think about birth parents with increasing frequency in adolescence as they struggle with the common question "Who am I?" How and when this becomes a decision to search will depend on the individual and may involve various stages, of varying length. For many adopted people, the decision-making process about whether or not to seek more information and contact birth relatives may take years. It is often not until their late 20s, and maybe later, that the search starts. In fact, the average age for people to search as reported in *Adoption, Search and Reunion* is 30.

In the first part of this chapter we begin to explore what motivates some adopted people to search and others not to search. The research reported in *Adoption, Search and Reunion* gives an insight into the triggers that result in adoptive people searching for information from adoption records and then making contact with birth relatives. This chapter also looks at the particular situation faced by "foundlings" where no information on their origins exists.

What research tells us

In *Adoption, Search and Reunion*, when searchers were asked what spurred them on to make contact with The Children's Society, which had placed them for adoption, over 82 per cent said that it was because they had a long-standing curiosity about their origins. Seventy-seven per cent said that they wanted to know more about themselves, 69 per cent wanted background information, and nearly 50 per cent wanted information so that they could begin a search for their birth family.

The majority of both searchers and non-searchers reported thinking about their birth family at some point when growing up. Eighty-five per cent of them often wondered what their birth parents (but particularly their birth mother) looked like and whether they shared any of their characteristics.

Not every adopted person who sought information from adoption records decided to embark on a search for their birth relatives. In fact, 15 per cent of the 394 adopted people surveyed had sought information about their adoption but decided to go no further. For them the information they received was enough to satisfy their curiosity or suggested to them that it was not the right time. Other reasons included being afraid that searching for and contacting the birth family would cause upset to their adoptive family. But for others, seeking information may only be a first step. Even when somebody says that information is all they want, they may go on to seek contact at some later stage. For the majority who seek information from adoption records, however, the main intention is to locate and make contact with birth relatives.

There are two relevant findings that distinguish searchers from non-searchers. First, searchers were more likely to describe relationships with their adoptive family and their overall experience of being adopted with mixed, or in a few cases, negative feelings. This suggests that ambivalent or negative feelings about one's adoptive family might be one of the motivating factors to begin an active search for information and birth relatives. But 53 per cent of searchers described their adoption as being a positive experience, which shows that the motivations for searching or not are much more complex than simply being happy or not about the adoption. For example, an adopted person may feel very loved and happy with their adoptive parents, having a deep sense of belonging, but may feel ambivalent about their adoptive status. The decision to search or not therefore needs to be seen within the context of the fact that many adopted adults have a natural curiosity about their origins and want more information about their birth family.

The second distinguishing finding is that half of non-searchers (47 per cent in total) said that they had no curiosity about their origins or background and, thus, did not feel a need to search for their birth relatives. Some of the reasons given were to do with not wanting to upset their adoptive parents or being afraid of finding out information that would be upsetting for themselves. But while the other half of non-searchers were curious, they too thought that searching might distress their adoptive parents or themselves.

Many searchers have firm ideas about what they are looking for even before they receive information from their adoption records. For example, 75 per cent wanted to contact their birth mother; 40 per cent wanted to meet a birth brother or sister; and 38 per cent had decided that it was their birth father whom they wanted to find. Eleven per cent wanted to find as many birth relatives as they could – birth mother, father and brothers and sisters and possibly others too. But once the search was underway, and given the amount of information available, 91 per cent decided that their birth mother would be the first person whom they wished to find.

What do these adults hope for or fear when they embark on their search? Searchers reported a variety of expectations, not all mutually exclusive. Sixty per cent said that they believed that they would be happier for it; 53 per cent worried about being rejected; and half (50 per cent) worried that they would be unsuccessful. Thirty-five per cent said that they hoped to have a meaningful relationship with the birth relative, 20 per cent thought that their birth relative had been waiting for them to contact and 11 per cent believed that they would be able to find a birth relative quickly.

Not surprisingly, 66 per cent reported feelings of nervousness, 52 per cent excitement and 41 per cent uncertainty. →

Why adopted adults search

Curiosity is a basic human characteristic and curiosity about who we are and where we came from is a significant part of this. It is not surprising, therefore, that one of the findings from *Adoption, Search and Reunion* is that adopted people reported that they had a long-standing curiosity about their origins and wanted information to help them with this. It is estimated that well over half the people who have been adopted will make some enquiries and effort to search for information about their origins and then attempt to make contact with a birth relative.

When adopted adults know that they have a genetic history that involves people other than their adoptive parents and family, then it is understandable that they develop a curiosity about those who share that history. As *Adoption, Search and Reunion* shows, this does not always necessarily reflect how happy or otherwise one might have been in the adoptive family.

Heather, a searcher, believes that most adopted people will feel curious at one point in their lives, although they may not do anything about it:

> *I defy most children who have grown up in a family alternative to their birth one to not have some niggling curiosity; whether or not you decide to scratch it or ease that curiosity, it's very much up to you.*

The reasons for searching are almost as many as those who embark on a search. For some, like Craig, it was good old-fashioned curiosity, as well as a need to establish his racial identity, which impelled his search. But he did not start thinking about his birth parents until he had left home. Andrew too described how he has always been curious:

> *The adoption was successful and I had a very happy childhood – but I was always curious about my origins.*

But there may be other strong factors, apart from curiosity, which determine the wish to search. One is a need for a more complete sense of identity. Even someone who has had a very happy childhood with adoptive parents and in an adoptive family where they felt secure may still feel the need to establish the other dimensions to their sense of identity. Finding out *why* they look the way they do and why they may have certain talents or characteristics that are not shared by the adoptive family can be important if they are to make sense of these differences.

As a black woman who had been adopted in a white family, Koshii experienced both the need to understand her roots and also, when she herself became a parent, to be able to talk about her side of the birth family:

> *... my reasons for searching were not really to do with being unhappy or trying to find an alternative family ... I'd had children of my own by the time I took a definite decision to start searching and I felt uncomfortable about not being able to talk about my side of the*

*family. I could see the traits that came from their [her children's]
father but I couldn't honestly say what came from me and that hurt –
like the birth.*

*The desire to know where I came from grew, so that when people
asked me where I came from I could tell them I wanted to know who I
looked like. If I did look like someone else, was it my mum, was it my
dad or even my grandparents? I wanted to know about my
mannerisms, the way I walked ... but most of all I wanted the other
piece of the jigsaw about my heritage.*

Heather echoed this need and the importance of having some basic information
about herself:

*As I got to my teens, I thought I might search one day. When I was 18,
I applied for the information that was around my birth, but then I
decided not to do anything about the searching immediately after
that. I kept a diary in my teens and I must have had some massive crisis
at one stage about being adopted because I wrote pages and pages,
and I was scared my mum and dad would find out so I tippexed it out
... I was probably feeling a bit unloved, but I know all teenagers go
through that, and I know I wasn't unloved ... in a sense, getting the
information had sorted out that immediate crisis – about who I was
and where I came from – because I really had no information at all. I
didn't know how much I weighed, the hospital where I was born,
what my name was, anything like that, and that was, in a way, quite
enough to deal with at the time. I wanted to know more about my
birth parents, but I think it was really more about me, more than
thinking about the reasons why it never worked out and why I was
adopted ... the sheet I got was fairly basic information, but at the
time it was enough. (A, S&R, pp. 40–41)*

Another reason adopted adults search for information is to try and understand the
reasons why they were placed for adoption – not out of any animosity towards their
birth mother (most adopted adults understand the enormous struggle their birth
mother must have been through before placing their baby for adoption) but out of
compassion that a woman could find herself in such a situation. Some adopted
people just want to let the birth mother know that they have had a happy life and
that adoption was a good decision in the circumstances.

Heather, who speaks on the video, had thought about searching for many years but
had never quite managed to take that first step until she saw a television
programme about adoption. It was about birth mothers and one woman said that,
if she had murdered her son 30 years ago, she would be out of prison by now but
she remained in a prison of her own making by having had her son adopted, so
that she could give him a better start in life. This had made Heather really think
about the position that her birth mother had been placed in years ago. Heather
said that she realised at this point that it was beholden upon her to let her birth
mother out of prison: 'If there was any chink of light to say: "Hello, I'm well"', as

→

she put it, then she needed to let her know that she was alive, well and that she had made the right decision.

So some adopted people may be prompted to search by a television programme or newspaper article. Others may have met someone who had searched. Others still may need to know about their medical history or, as with Craig and Koshii, to know more about their racial identity.

For some adopted people the feeling that they did not belong may be the reason for them seeking out their birth family, as in the case of Nina:

> ... the feeling grew throughout my teens that this family would never belong to me, as opposed to at the beginning vague feeling of uneasiness that I don't belong anywhere ... that I didn't fit in, that I have never fitted in. (A, S&R, p. 93)

Martine said:

> I always felt ... I didn't feel I belonged, not because of the way I was treated but because I was so different. (A, S&R, p. 101)

Adopted people who do not search

But there are also people who choose not to search. Why? Do some adopted adults feel more settled in their adoptive families than others? *Adoption, Search and Reunion* showed that non-searchers were indeed less curious and had fewer questions about why they were adopted. Liz says:

> As I got older in my late teens, a few friends started to say to me, 'Aren't you interested in finding out who your real parents are?' And I always used to say, 'No, not really. Why should I?' I was totally happy with my current family – so there wasn't a need as far as I was concerned ... that's not to say that I might not have done as I've got older but there wasn't ever a time when I seriously thought about looking for her or finding out any more information. (A, S&R, p. 58)

Jane, who 'thought about it [searching] very briefly', said:

> But it seemed to me that just being curious wasn't a good enough reason to disrupt lots of lives ...

Perhaps the strongest lack of curiosity was shown by Carol, who was placed by The Children's Society and later came to work there:

> My thoughts about searching are that I don't particularly want to. I know that the information would be fairly readily available. In fact, at

one stage in my place of work I was so near to where my records were I could walk past the cupboard and touch them.

Anna is a non-searcher. She was adopted at six months old and has two older brothers, who are the birth children of her adoptive parents. Adoption was always 'very much out in the open' in her family. She never felt different from other family members. It may be that feeling not so different from the rest of the family is an important factor that makes searching feel less important. In Anna's words:

> *The experience of growing up adopted I think ... I didn't realise it was any different to anybody else's experience in the village where I grew up. I felt no different – I had a mum and a dad like everybody else and it was not particularly referred to.*

Anna, who calls herself 'statistically a non-searcher' – her mother contacted her when Anna was 24 – rarely thought about her birth father. She did think about her birth mother but only from the latter's perspective – how strange it must be for her to have a daughter whom she did not know. But she felt no resentment; indeed, she was grateful to that 17-year-old mother:

> *I knew she was only 17 years old, but in those days she probably wouldn't have been able to give me a good a start in life as I had ... so I saw it from a very positive view [of her].*

Jane is another non-searcher. She could always talk to her adoptive mother and brother (who is also adopted) about adoption but not to her father: 'I'm his little girl'. She had thought about her birth parents but her adoptive father and mother would be hurt if she chose to search. However, she also thought that if she decided to do so, they would both support her.

Jane says that her brother is even less interested in searching for his birth parents than she is.

Other non-searchers have also described how they would not want to search for fear of upsetting their adoptive parents.

Michelle says:

> *My parents, they did speak about it, like 'If you ever want to get in touch with your parents you can. It won't hurt us.' Well, they said that. But I thought deep down that it could hurt them. And I always sat there and thought, 'Who do I look like?' But I've never had the actual guts to get up and do it, you know. (A, S&R, pp. 59–60)*

Jessica could be described as a non-searcher although she did, in fact, make some enquiries when she was 18:

When I was 18 I took that opportunity then to start trying to trace my natural mother ... On the second meeting with him [the social worker] he actually had a piece of paper with the details surrounding the circumstances of my adoption. I always remember it was rather impersonal and upsetting at the time. It just basically said my mother was 5ft 5ins, brown hair, brown eyes, an art student – the putative father was blonde, there was also a note about my mother, at the time when she was carrying me, that she had actually attempted to commit suicide – and it all sounded really quite traumatic and sad. I decided then that it was just too big a thing for me to take on board and especially as the circumstances seemed quite traumatic for my natural mother. I started thinking, 'Maybe it's not right for me just to turn up in her life so many years later' – so I thought I'd just leave it. (A, S&R, p. 58)

Others, like Carol, did not particularly think about their birth parents when growing up because, as she said:

They belonged to a different era of which I was not a part.

Non-searchers did not share the same desire as adopted adults who initiate a search for information and seek contact with birth relatives. Carol had always known as a child that she was adopted because her adoptive parents were open about it even if they did not have much information. Her curiosity has not deepened over the years but she does know that information is available if she wants it. She has found it interesting to talk with people who have a "burning desire" to know and find birth relatives, although she does not share this desire. After meeting with a man who felt this way, she said that she was glad she did not have to share the man's 'deep-seated unhappiness' that the curiosity about one's origins and need to find one's birth parent causes. Her 'curiosity remained just curiosity'.

Carol says:

I have a set of parents and if I found my birth parents they would not be my parents – they would be other people. What would be the purpose, what would I gain? What would they gain?

If her birth parents made a search for her she said she would be 'taken aback, surprised and [I would] ask: "Why?"' It would *not* be her instinctive reaction to meet them.

Where adoption does affect Carol is in her lack of knowledge of her medical history. If she had a genetic illness she would have to have 'a deep think' about whether to search. Jane also agrees with Carol about this:

I have thought about trying ... well not trying to find medical history but I have thought about the implications of it and maybe if I knew I was going to have – I don't know, glaucoma or something like that –

lives | Sandy

then at least I would know to look out for it.

There are also those adopted adult non-searchers who do not search because of the one factor that also affects searchers – the fear that they may be rejected. This subject is considered in a later chapter.

The foundling: when there is no information to find

The term "foundling" is used for babies who have been abandoned (albeit usually in a safe place) by their birth mother with no identifying information. Unlike other children who are placed for adoption, they do not have the opportunity to obtain the basic details about their family background. They may well have been placed through an adoption agency, but that agency will not have obtained the information normally given by the birth mother at the time of the adoption. This means that they will not be able to embark on a search for birth relatives as other adopted people can, since they cannot have the identifying information they need to help them to do so.

The Children Act 1975 made a provision for a register of the births of children who had been abandoned, and whose parentage was unknown, to be compiled and held at the General Register Office. Since 1977, when this register came into being, there have been a total of 195 babies abandoned. Like other people, foundlings are issued with a birth certificate but this does not provide any information about the child's date of birth or his or her parents. Foundlings, therefore, do not have the opportunity to search for or discover what may seem inconsequential details about their birth and family background. Sandy remembers when she first enquired about her background:

> I can't remember any discussion about the background till I was late in my teens and that's when my older sister – who's two years older than me – wanted to find out about her origins and my parents were able to tell her the names, where her family actually came from – which was about ten minutes up the road and they could have

Sandy is a foundling – a deserted infant of unknown parents. Found on the steps of *Reynolds News*, near King's Cross station in the autumn of 1955, she was taken to a children's home and subsequently placed for adoption at about six months of age. Always knowing she was adopted, it was in her late teens that she became aware of her origins and the lack of information about herself. She is a nurse but now works with foundlings and also with parents whose children have been placed for adoption. She is married with three children.

Sandy initiated a support group for other foundlings and has tried to raise the profile of the effects of an abandonment, which sadly still occurs today.

→

> *virtually knocked on the door. At the time I then asked about my*
> *origins and was told in fact they had so little information except to*
> *say I'd been left on a doorstep near King's Cross in London.*

But she recalls that at that time the fact that there was no information did not bother her particularly as it was before 1975 and no adopted adults had access to any information about themselves. The law made it very difficult for any adopted person to find out about their origins and all adopted people were in the same boat. But the Children Act 1975 changed all that – it gave all adopted adults the right to have access to information, except for a minority – foundlings. This is something Sandy finds 'extremely frustrating'. She adds:

> *I really cannot remember how old I was – except I was in my late teens – it*
> *obviously did have an impact but for some reason I just can't remember*
> *my age at the time. But I do remember at the time it didn't make a lot of*
> *difference to myself, as at that period adopted people couldn't search*
> *anyhow. Because I knew it was previous to 1976 that I was told – so in a*
> *way I was on an equal footing with other adopted people.*

Unlike a non-searcher, who is in a position to choose whether or not they want to discover information about their history, a foundling is just not able to do so. To quote Sandy again:

> *As a foundling I have no knowledge of my medical health. Now that*
> *didn't matter back in the '50s because you just didn't know when you*
> *were adopted. But as I've got older there is more development of*
> *medical science – if I knew there was a family history of breast cancer I*
> *could perhaps be screened. That's something that I am denied it seems*
> *because I am an adopted person. In the future the babies that are left*
> *today will face those exact dilemmas except it might be more difficult*
> *because by then there will be a medical assessment done that they*
> *may not be able to routinely access.*

Foundlings will, often literally, have been found, having been placed somewhere – a church, a telephone kiosk – where they were intended to be discovered. Sometimes their link with their past will be something which may appear to a non-foundling as mundane – but to them, significant – for example, their name being associated with where they were found. Sandy was named Elizabeth Gray – after the new monarch and London's Gray's Inn Road where she was found. Many foundlings may not know their date of birth, let alone the time they were born. Most people do not regard information about their star sign as very important and neither does Sandy – until it comes up in casual conversation. For people like Sandy or other adopted people who have been adopted from overseas where information about their personal history and birth family may not be available, the lack of information can be extremely frustrating:

> *Not being able to find out information about your origins is extremely*
> *frustrating. Apart from the fact that the system doesn't seem to be set*

up to support adult foundlings, of which I am one. It just doesn't make it easy for you to get information – even the little bit of information there is, there seem to be a lot of brick walls you come up against. And even at the end of the day you know there's not going to be much, but somehow to think that somebody might select what you might need and send it to you in a letter does not seem right. I hope that doesn't happen any more.

After her first child was born, Sandy did her utmost to find whatever details about her origins might be available. It was then that she learned the time and date of when she was found. Like any other adopted person, Sandy sought information about herself. What she received, after counselling by a social worker, was a certificate, which recorded when and where she was found. Her birth mother and father are listed as "unknown". She said:

That was very interesting to me because I had always had an idea where I was found but I never knew the date or time. And for the first time I was actually seeing it in black and white. And that was quite a moving moment.

It was also when Sandy had her own children that she saw the similarities between herself and her children and, at the same time, the differences between herself, her sisters and her adoptive parents:

I struggle to find similarities with my adoptive family – it wasn't until I had my own children that I now see the similarities that I perhaps looked for but couldn't find. My adoptive mother used to say that I was like members of her family – but it never really quite rang true. Because I suppose I knew it wasn't true – and whilst I have my own children now, it's only now that I see, for instance, the way that my daughter stands, it's just like me, and I used to say to my husband, who I've known since I was 15, when we used to walk along the road, I used to look at families and say, 'Aren't they alike?' and my husband used to say, 'Of course they're alike, they're related.' And I think when you're not in that situation, it is hard to understand perhaps that those things are missing. Not from all adoptive families, obviously, but from some they are. And I don't think I ever really felt I quite fitted in somehow.

The neglect of foundlings in the adoption literature is mirrored by the lack of support for adult foundlings. It is important to acknowledge the particular position of those who cannot trace any information about their birth parents and families. There is, for example, no standardised collection of information about foundlings apart from that held at the General Register Office. Sandy says:

It is crucial that everything is kept, everything recorded, everything shared.

→

Questions

☐ What are three important reasons for searching?

☐ What are three important reasons for not searching?

☐ Describe some of the differences between people who search and people who do not search?

☐ Is there such a thing as a true non-searcher?

☐ How much do you agree with Jane in the video that 'just being curious' is not enough reason to search?

Exercises

Show clips from the video of the adopted people who searched and then have a small group discussion.

Adoptive parents

Describe some of the fears and anxieties your adult adopted son/ daughter might have about starting to search, particularly in relation to you and their relationship with you and/or fears about what they might find out about their birth family.

Adopted people

What help and support do you think adopted people need from the adoptive family, partners, friends and adoption counsellors in making decisions about searching?

Adoption professionals

Think about what motivates adopted people to search or not. In addition to natural curiosity about origins, there may be additional factors including:

○ feeling different

○ a feeling of not belonging

○ wanting to find someone who looks like yourself

○ wishing to develop a relationship with one's birth family

Think about the impact these different motives might have for

○ the adopted adult

○ the adoptive parent

○ the birth parent

3

The journey begins: preparing to search

THE JOURNEY BEGINS

Introduction

Many adopted people describe how they have thought about searching for more information about their background or contacting birth relatives for several years before they have been able to pluck up enough courage to take action. Some adopted people just want to get background information and no more, while others will want to make contact. But, whatever pathway is taken, there will be implications not just for the adopted person but also for their birth and adoptive families as well as other significant people in their lives – especially if they have or want to consider having a family of their own. There are many questions that adopted adults ask themselves. They will want to know how their adoptive parents will react. Will they be supportive? Will they regard the idea of searching as a betrayal? Will they see this as a breach within the family? Should they tell their adoptive family about their desire to search?

In this chapter we look at the process of beginning a search for adoption records and birth family members, and the role that counselling and intermediary services play.

What research tells us

If a person was adopted before 12 November 1975 and is not aware of their original name, then they have to contact the General Registrar at the Office for National Statistics to make an application for access to birth records. An arrangement will then be made for the adopted person to see an adoption counsellor, who will make an appointment to meet the adopted person before identifying information is passed on that will enable them to apply for a copy of their original birth certificate.

When adopted people already know their original birth name, they can apply for a copy of their birth certificate. Some adopted people not only know their original name but also the agency which placed them. In these circumstances, adopted people will often approach the adoption agency themselves to ask for the background information held about them on the agency's adoption records. Most adoption agencies would, however, expect a practitioner to meet with the adopted person to discuss the implications of receiving background information from the agency records, rather than simply handing over the details relating to the adoption and family background.

This discussion would include explaining the possible outcomes of what the person wanted to do. The overwhelming majority of searchers do take this route. Most

→

people value the opportunity to discuss their position with an adoption social worker prior to and during the search. They can find it helpful to meet someone who understands, has an insight into and will provide support during the search and reunion process. Meeting the adoption counsellor can also be important as it gives the adopted person the opportunity to talk about their hopes, fears and expectations. It also gives them a chance to think about the implications of receiving information and any subsequent action they may or may not wish to take, such as beginning a search for birth relatives and making contact with them.

As stated previously, sixty-seven per cent of searchers felt that they had either always known that they were adopted or were under the age of five when told this by their adoptive parents. However, a majority of both searchers (70 per cent) and non-searchers (74 per cent) did not feel comfortable seeking information about their birth parents or their origins from their adoptive parents; 56 per cent of searchers and 61 per cent of non-searchers felt that they were given no or very little background information by adoptive parents about their adoption. Sometimes this was because the adoptive parents did not know much or they chose not to reveal what they knew.

Sixty per cent of searchers felt that the result of the search would make them happier but 53 per cent worried about being rejected. Others felt charged with determination, even anger, feeling that they had a moral right to be seen by their birth relative. Half of them worried that the search would be unsuccessful. When they anticipated the search, most people described a mixture of feeling nervous (66 per cent), excited (52 per cent) and unsure (41 per cent). A small number said they were calm, even matter of fact, but the majority were in a heightened emotional state. A small number said that they felt some disloyalty towards their adoptive parents.

The preparation

Often adopted people are really surprised when they discover that there may be background information that they can have access to. Heather described 'another floodgate' opening when she telephoned The Children's Society (her adoptive parents had given her the name of the adoption agency) to find that it held her records.

When they contemplate searching, adopted people are often acutely aware of other people's feelings. They may have thought about searching for a long time but put it off, fearing that it would cause hurt and upset to either their adoptive family or their birth family or both. When a decision has been made to search for birth relatives, some adopted people prefer to be in total control of their own search, while others prefer to work in partnership with the adoption counsellor and share some of the tasks in locating the birth relative.

Most adopted people are particularly sensitive to the feelings of their adoptive and birth families. As Moira says:

I did think about searching. I thought I'd do it when I was older, like when I was 18. And then when I reached 18, I thought, 'no, I'll put up for a little bit longer'. I never actually plucked up the courage to do it. I just didn't know where to start … but I did want to. And I didn't want to upset my mum and dad and I didn't want to be rejected by my birth mother. (A, S&R, p. 58)

Nimmy, who is a searcher, delayed her decision to do so for years because she did not want to "rock the boat". She believed that her adoptive family would feel rejected if she searched. Her mother, she said, 'was nervous but she is a mother and a daughter so she understood'.

However, once the decision has been made and the process begun, adopted people can experience a range of feelings from excitement to sadness, joy to anger. Having the chance to share these feelings can be very important and can help the adopted person to keep in context their own experience and that of other adopted people.

Nimmy thinks that:

It is all the better if you can make it [the search] a family experience.

For Andrew, there had been excitement at the prospect of meeting his mother:

I couldn't believe I was going to meet someone with whom I had a genetic link.

This led to 'a very strong and instant bond'.

Something of the same happened with Nimmy who says:

… having been brought up in a family where my adoptive parents had three children of their own – they had two, then adopted two and then had another one – it had always fascinated me that they looked like each other and so on. And so for me to have someone who was my own flesh and blood was extraordinary.

How people prepare differs enormously. Some will talk to lots of people – their adoptive family, partners, children and friends. Some people talk to no one: they ponder the prospect alone. Many prepare by doing a lot of research – they try to find how others have met the same challenge. They may read books about search and reunion or join a support group for adopted people.

Counselling and intermediary services

Thinking about birth relatives and whether or not to make contact with them is not usually a spur of the moment decision, but often something that has been thought

→

about for several years, either in a conscious or subconscious way. David, a searcher, explains:

> I started my search when I was 34 ... I nearly did it when I was a teenager, 16/17. Got very close to it and I think I used to think, 'I'm going to find out'. But I'm glad I didn't really because I wouldn't have been able to handle it then. If I'd done it at 16, I'd have fucked up everything, no question about it. I'd have blown my adoptive parents away, I'd have screwed myself up. Then every year after Christmas and my birthday I thought about doing it – and it took another 20 years to do it. (A, S&R, p. 53)

But making the first step to find either information from adoption records or seek out birth relatives can take enormous courage as the adopted person is entering unknown territory. The fear of what the outcome may be can prevent people from taking that first step. Charlotte says:

> My adoptive parents never brought up the subject of adoption because I never brought it up – and they thought I didn't want to know, that I had no interest. And vice versa ... I didn't think it was a good idea to search ... I didn't know if I was protecting myself more than her [birth mother] or vice versa – a combination of the two I think. It was 'I want to know' but overridden by 'I don't want to know in case I don't like it' or 'she might not like it'. And always in the background, concern that I might hurt my adoptive parents – they were marvellous and still are – I'd never felt this need to understand and know about my roots. (A, S&R, p. 60)

But as in Heather's case, once she had decided to seek information from records, she was met with an acceptance that took her by surprise. Until then, the word "adoption" had felt taboo:

> So, it was a quick 192 on the telephone: 'Please can I have the headquarters of The Children's Society?'. I was put in touch, instantly, with someone who said, almost in the first sentence: 'Yeah, we've got your records'. Another floodgate opened – someone for whom adoption was not a dirty word, someone who said 'yes' in the same sentence as 'adoption'.

Meeting the counsellor

It is accepted practice that in most adoption agencies an adopted person would meet with an adoption practitioner or counsellor before being given any information held on the adoption agency's record. Receiving information from records can, as we have heard, be a positive experience as it can fill in the gaps in an adopted person's past personal history. Not every adoption agency, though, will have complete records. Some records may have been destroyed over the years, either through fire or

lives | Carol

flooding or because it was felt that they were no longer needed. Indeed, where the adoption has been arranged privately and where an agency has not been involved, there may be a lack of information.

David, a non-searcher who was contacted by the adoption agency to let him know that his birth mother wanted to make contact, decided to meet his counsellor so that he could see the records and understand the reasons for his adoption. He was taken aback by the amount of information available and also by the fact that his adoptive father had written to the adoption agency to say how proud he and his wife were of their new son. David explains:

> We continued to exchange letters ...
> meanwhile, while I was on holiday, I visited
> the society because I wanted to see my file.
> And that was my point of contact. So one
> day we drove from the South coast up to
> the society and I went through my file with
> one of my social workers there – and I must
> have been in the office about three hours –
> it was a bit of a marathon because I only
> had one go at it. And I got all the copies of
> it – some of it had been damaged in a
> flood apparently. I'd heard about this flood
> and some of my papers ... but the beauty
> of bureaucracy is that things tend to be
> repeated on forms, so if a piece of
> information isn't on one form it can be on
> another, in perhaps a slightly different
> category.
> And we found most of it – perhaps the
> most moving thing for me of that was
> letters from my father, my adoptive father,
> I found in there. And they did move me, I
> have to say that it did make me rather
> emotional. My adoptive father had written
> how glad they were to have me, and what
> a difference it had made to both of them.
> And growing up, of course, I suppose I saw
> us as a large family but then it was just the
> three of us. And I suppose I hadn't realised
> the impact I'd made on them. I found that
> a very emotional moment.

Many adopted people have found the counselling and

Carol was adopted in 1958 when she was less than six months old, and is an only child. She describes her childhood as happy. She has decided that she does not want to receive any further details about her adoption or embark on a search for birth relatives. Carol works as a finance and administration director for a charitable trust.

She speaks about the reasons why she has no desire to find out further information about her origins.

→

preparation process really helpful, as the adoption counsellor can be there providing the support or the validation of feelings that other adopted people express. As Nimmy says:

> I got fantastic support from my counsellor and we went through all the possibilities really of what could happen to you because you might think 'Oh! Wow! This will be such a wonderful reunion' or 'Oh, it will be terrible'. But there are so many things to consider. Whether your mother might not be alive – or your mother might be mad – your parent (whichever parent you are searching for) could be ill, terminally ill ... all sorts of things that I hadn't really considered and I was really supported in thinking about what all the possibilities could be before setting off on that journey, and I think that was important.

For others, meeting with a counsellor helped them to move forward with the search feeling more confident and knowledgeable with how to go about it. As David, a searcher (to be distinguished from David who appears in the video and is a non-searcher), says:

> By nature I am very committed to things. If I do them, I do them 100 per cent. The best thing about visiting Laura, the counsellor at The Children's Society, and initiating the search was that it enabled me to move on to the next step. Prior to meeting her, it was unknown. There were just these two people out there who I'd had some information on for a long time, but never really taken any further. The meeting and then the search filled in a lot of blanks. (A, S&R, p. 53)

Sometimes people need to seek further counselling as they struggle through the lifelong issues raised by adoption. Nimmy had a positive response from her birth father but a negative one from her mother. Although she felt she had dealt with the rejection, a few years on this came to the surface again:

> I think it's important to get some counselling support and that's what I got through The Children's Society at every turn. There's always somebody at the end of the phone if I feel the need to speak with someone. And I remember after about three or four years after trying to trace my mother, issues came up about it again and I felt a bit foolish about ringing up but my phone call was warmly welcomed and there was someone there for me right away – just helping me through.
>
> It's nice to know that other people do go through these experiences and through having someone as a counsellor. I find that you hear about what other people go through and you get a sense of not being alone – and that you're not crazy because you are going through it that way too ... It's important, I think, to have someone to talk to about it, especially if you are busy judging yourself for the way you feel about the experience.

Making contact: using an intermediary

The vast majority of adopted people (78 per cent) do not make direct contact with the birth relative, but tend to prefer to use an intermediary, usually the adoption social worker or counsellor whom they have met to gain access to their adoption records. An advantage of using an intermediary is that they will be in a position to help the birth relative who has been approached to work through some of their initial feelings to enable them to come to a decision about how to respond. An intermediary can also provide a "buffer" in cases where the contact has been met with a negative response. An experienced intermediary can also give adopted people information about the average length of time it takes for a birth relative to respond, as well as other aspects of the contact process. Heather recalls:

> *Well, the contact letter went out – we'd verified the address – and I was warned by my counsellor that this could take a fair amount of time. I thought it was fair to contact first by letter and I was warned that, at the end of the day, the person could be on holiday, could be in hospital, may not want to reply ... 101 reasons. So I was braced for a good many weeks. As it was, it was only 24 hours. But during that 24 hours I managed to cry my way through boxes of tissues, be physically ill – shake, shiver, sweat and carry on – I had no idea how long ... if this had gone on for weeks there would have been nothing left for them to have found!*
>
> *Back came the reply and I got a phone call from my counsellor one evening that said, 'listen to this' and she played her answerphone message and it basically said, 'Yes, I'm Heather's mother, I do want contact'. Now once I'd stopped howling ... and I'm not a crying person ... but once I'd stopped howling, the impact came through. I had to have it played several times so that I believed it – great!*

Using an intermediary to make the first contact can also give time for the person being contacted to gain more information and to gather their thoughts and feelings before they make a decision to take the contact forward, either to exchange information directly with the adopted person or to arrange a meeting. The intermediary can help the adopted person and the birth relative negotiate the next steps in a safer and a realistic way.

People vary in how and when a meeting should take place. Some people like to take on the arrangements and meet on their own while others, like Sarah, want their counsellor to be present:

> *I wanted to take Kate [her counsellor] with me although I had Anna [her daughter] with me as well. Anna was eight months old. I wanted somebody else there ... when we went inside she [mother] just burst into tears and Kate said, 'What do you think?' And Vera said: 'Oh, she's beautiful.' (A, S&R, p. 116)*

Although it is important that adopted people feel that they are in control of the →

situation and can make decisions which are right for them, having an adoption counsellor can help the adopted person and, of course, the adoptive parents and birth relatives to feel supported along the journey of contact and reunion.

Some adopted people do not want to use an intermediary but want to manage the arrangements themselves. This was the case with Hazel:

> *Once I found her, I went for it. Because the more I thought about it, the more scared I got and thought, 'No, I can't wait, I've got to do it.' I phoned her up. I got to the last digit of the number and I thought – I put it down six times – and I thought, 'No, I'm going to do it this time' and eventually I phoned her up and she came on the phone ... And I said, 'You don't know me, you know me as Helen Jones' and it went absolutely quiet and I said, 'Hello, are you still there?' And she went: 'Oh my God!' So she said, 'How are you?' and I said, 'I'm fine' and she said, 'I've been waiting. I thought this day might come,' and she asked how long I had been looking and I said, 'A long while.' And she said, 'Are you married?' and she started off asking me questions and I said, 'I've got questions to ask you' and she said, 'How about coming up here to meet me – come to my house?' And so we arranged to meet the following week at her home, which frightened me even more. So I went up and met her. It was quite an experience because she's not how I thought she would look. She's quite a nice lady. (A, S&R, p. 52)*

Susie felt similarly:

> *I wanted to do the contacting myself. Because ... I don't know ... I didn't want her really to have a choice ... I was going to meet her no matter what by this time. It took me four years to do it and I didn't want to put myself in a situation of meeting my blood mother or father and being rejected. I wasn't going to give her a chance to reject me because at the end of the day all I wanted was answers to my questions. I think everybody that's adopted already feels slightly rejected and a rejection like that must be another rejection. There was no intention of having a relationship whatsoever because I've got my parents, my parents have always been there for me, and if they hadn't been behind me ... I wouldn't have bothered. (A, S&R, p. 52)*

What is important is that adopted people have the opportunity to think through the pluses and minuses of making a direct or an indirect approach using an intermediary. Given the potential consequences for all involved, thinking it through before taking action is very important.

Questions

☐ What are the advantages and disadvantages of meeting with an adoption counsellor prior to receiving information from adoption records and embarking on a search for birth relatives?

☐ If you were counselling an adopted person who wanted to find information or embark on a search for birth relatives, how would you prepare them? What issues do you think they would need to address?

☐ What support and services are needed for adopted people who decide to search?

☐ Why is it important for adopted people to have information and a sense of connection with the birth family?

☐ Why might the adoptive family feel rejected by an adopted person's decision to search?

☐ What reasons might there be for not telling adoptive parents until after the search has been successfully completed or even not telling at all?

☐ What relationship (if any) would you expect to build for yourself with the birth family?

☐ What practical information does an adopted person need to have to begin a search?

☐ How could you help adopted people with their search?

Exercises

For adoption counsellors in small groups or pairs:

○ What immediate feelings are raised in you about adopted people who want to seek information about their background history and begin a search for birth family members?

○ What are the worst possible fears an adopted person might have about their past?

○ Describe some of the challenges that are presented for the adoption counsellor when counselling an adopted adult and sharing information from adoption records.

○ How can you ensure that your agency offers services that do not discriminate against people who have a physical disability, mental illness or learning difficulties?

→

Exercises continued

Card exercise for adoption counsellors

On each card write a different scenario and in small groups consider:

○ what you would feel

○ what an adopted person might feel

○ what you could say to the adopted person

Suggested scenarios

○ A child of rape or incest

○ No name of the father

○ Specific issues about the mother which might concern her mental health or criminal status

○ No background information because the adopted person is a foundling

○ The birth mother has written to the adoption agency to say in no circumstances must she be contacted.

○ An adopted adult had an unhappy adoption and now wants to find the birth family as they believe this would enable them to find true happiness and have the family experience they never had.

○ The adoption agency or local authority has lost or destroyed all the papers relating to the adoption and adopted person's family history.

○ An adopted person has been diagnosed as a paranoid schizophrenic. They are distressed after receiving information from the adoption records and you fear that they may go straight to the last known address of the birth mother.

○ An adopted person has been told a different story to that which you have on the file.

○ There is confidential information on file about the birth family which the birth mother had said she never wanted to be shared with her child.

Small group discussion

○ How do you set up the counselling interview?

○ What particular issues do you consider?

○ What might be the expectations of the adopted person about this interview?

○ At what stage would you share information from the adoption records with the adopted person?

For discussion

When sharing confidential background information from adoption records, discuss how you can balance the tensions created by the decisions about whom the information belongs to. What is third party information and when should adopted people not be given access to information about other

Exercises continued

members of their birth or adoptive family? What matters would you share with the adopted person?

A suggested list

○ The birth mother has had other children placed for adoption.

○ The birth mother had an abortion before conceiving the adopted person.

○ The paternal grandfather was imprisoned for incest.

○ The maternal grandmother had been in prison and the birth mother had a short spell of being in care.

○ The birth mother was adopted.

○ A letter from the adoptive parents, who were having second thoughts about adopting, described how they could not feel any real affection but the adoption nevertheless went ahead.

○ The birth mother had a history of mental illness and tried to commit suicide when she was 18 years old.

○ The birth mother was raped.

Debate: to what extent should the intermediary take an active role in searching and actually undertake some of the work?

For: What will be the advantages?

Against: What will be the disadvantages?

○ for you as the intermediary

○ for the adopted person

○ for the birth parent

○ for the adoptive parents

4

OUT OF THE BLUE

"Out of the blue": what happens when birth relatives make contact

Introduction

Adoption, Search and Reunion included 78 adopted people who had decided not to make a search for birth relatives, but had been approached through The Children's Society's intermediary service to let them know of a birth relative's enquiry and desire for contact.

There is significant evidence (Feast and Smith, 1995 and 1993; Hughes and Logan, 1993; Howe *et al*, 1992; Winkler and Van Keppel, 1984) that the trauma for birth parents of giving up a child for adoption and the subsequent resolution of the loss can take many years. At a time when the social climate was such that illegitimacy and single parenthood (other than through widowhood) were something to be frowned upon, many birth mothers felt they had no choice but to place their child for adoption. During the 1990s, however, there was recognition of the position of birth mothers in particular, but also that of other birth relatives. This resulted in some adoption agencies providing an intermediary service for birth relatives who wanted to trace the adopted adult relative. Services have developed in a patchy and inconsistent way, but this is about to change with the new legislation enacted in England and Wales.

The Adoption and Children Act 2002 has recognised that adoption is something which lasts a lifetime for many birth relatives – mainly birth mothers, but also birth fathers, brothers and sisters and other family members. The new Act gives birth relatives of an adopted person the right to request an intermediary service so that they may let the adopted adult relative know of their interest for contact. No identifying information can be given to the birth relative without the adopted person's expressed permission. Although these are new legal provisions, many adopted people have already struggled with thoughts about how they might handle such an approach. As Carol says:

> *If my birth parents made an enquiry to the agency where I was adopted through – and presumably the agency then let me know such an enquiry has happened – I think I'd be rather taken aback in the first instance. I can see the first question would be 'Why?', which is a little defensive isn't it? I would be surprised and puzzled and possibly wanting to know why at this stage. I wouldn't be thinking 'oh yes'. It would be my instinctive reaction to think I will go out there and meet that enquirer.*

Jane also thought about this before the law was changed:

If they had made the effort to track me down I would think it was important for them and maybe I could ... I don't know ... be of comfort to them in some way ... but, yes, if they wanted to make the approach I wouldn't say no but I think that's unlikely now – I mean they've had quite a long time if they wanted to contact me and they haven't, so ...

What research tells us

One of the main reasons that adopted people gave in *Adoption, Search and Reunion* for not making enquiries about their background was because they were afraid it would upset their adoptive parents (44 per cent). People also said that they considered that their adoptive parents were their *real* parents (34 per cent); 31 per cent were scared that the information might be upsetting and 30 per cent said that they were not emotionally strong enough to begin a search for information or birth relatives.

Nearly half (47 per cent) of non-searchers said that they had not thought about contacting a birth relative, but 42 per cent had done so. Indeed, 21 per cent of all non-searchers in the sample had taken a preliminary step to try and contact a birth relative before The Children's Society had contacted them on behalf of one.

Seventy-six per cent of non-searchers, whatever their own reasons for not searching, thought that it was right for adoption agencies to let them know that a birth relative wanted to make contact. Only six per cent said it was definitely wrong and 18 per cent said they were unsure about whether it was a good idea to be told. And fewer than ten people (eight per cent) said that they would take action, if need be, to prevent a birth relative contacting them.

When a birth relative initiated a contact it was most likely to be the birth mother (71 per cent) but nearly a quarter of contacts were initiated by a birth brother or sister (23 per cent). Birth fathers were responsible for only three per cent of contacts.

The majority (90 per cent) of adopted people contacted in this way felt a mixture of two or more of the following: surprise, excitement, shock, curiosity and anxiety. A minority were angry or disturbed at being contacted and ten per cent of non-searchers chose not to have any direct contact with the birth relative.

Some of the reasons people gave for not wanting contact were to do with feeling uninterested in exchanging information, or that it was the wrong time, or that they did not want to upset their adoptive parents.

What happens when birth relatives make contact?

We have explored some of the reasons why adopted people make a decision not to search for information about birth relatives. We know that these can range from not wanting to upset their adoptive parent to being afraid of the information they might discover, to facing a possible rejection. So being contacted by a birth relative when not expected will inevitably raise particular feelings for those adopted people who had not considered ever initiating a search for birth relatives. Hearing about a birth relative's interest and desire for contact can place adopted people in a situation they may not be prepared for.

As we have noted, until the introduction of the Adoption and Children Act 2002, intermediary services for birth relatives were patchy. But now that intermediary services are about to be firmly set within a legislative framework, this may mean that adopted people and their adoptive parents will not be as surprised or shocked by an approach as some of the adopted people in the study, such as Alan:

> My initial reaction was: 'Jesus Christ!' Well, anyone would, wouldn't they? You get a letter out of the blue. 'Oh, jolly good!' You wouldn't be human if it didn't surprise you, would you? (A, S&R, p. 62)

Some people, like Brian, feel initial anger:

> The letter came direct to my mum and dad and, as luck had it, we were staying with them ... Sunday morning it was, they said, 'Here you are, there's this letter, have a read of that'. It really was out of the blue. It shocked us all right down to the ground but if anyone from The Children's Society had appeared, knocking on the front door that day, dad would have torn them limb from limb, I think, because it really did upset everybody. But I've talked about it since and I don't really think there's a different way of doing it – it's got to be done somehow – you can't have a complete stranger turning up on your doorstep saying 'hello'. But it was certainly very upsetting finding out, particularly for the parents. (A, S&R, p. 62)

Even people who do welcome being found can sometimes feel anger, confusion, upset, loneliness or depression when this happens. These emotions and a sense of being "invaded" go together with shock and feeling protective towards their adoptive family. Liz was one of those:

> I got the letter ... completely out of the blue ... I just read the first sentence and I knew who it was from, and it was such an enormous shock ... very, very upsetting ... It just completely threw me. I wasn't expecting it, I suppose. So I was completely unprepared and it was very upsetting and I was quite distressed by it – a whole range of emotions going through my mind, thinking: 'How dare she do this!"
>
> [After two or three weeks] I decided to write a letter back to her saying how I felt – that I was quite angry that she'd contacted me in this way. I'd always been very happy and content with my life and had no reason for wanting to contact her and that my family were devastated by what she'd done ... and 'there's no room for you in my life and I'd appreciate it if you didn't contact me again'. (A, S&R, p. 63)

Interestingly, four years later, the passing of time, curiosity and a boyfriend who asked Liz whether she didn't really want to know, caused her to contact her mother through an intermediary.

Others are more cautious. Michelle remembers:

> Well, it started off [when] The Children's Society sent my mum a letter asking if I was still at the address. My mum said yes – sent a photograph of me. And then mum, or was it me, got a letter through saying that my birth mum wanted to get in contact with me. And I was, 'Oh dear! Oh no! What do I do?' I was so nervous. Very tearful. But I thought, 'Why not?' Then I wrote a letter back saying, 'Yes, I'll get in contact with her through The Children's Society but not giving our addresses yet' – not quite yet. We started writing to each other for about a year and then she wrote her telephone number on top of one of her letters and said if I wanted to get in touch I could. And then one night I phoned her and I said, 'Hello – is Julia there?' And she said, 'Yeah' and I said, 'It's Michelle.' 'Michelle?' she went. I said, 'Your daughter!' And that was it – cor! Screamed down my ear and she was excited. She started crying. That was it. I started crying ... so the week after that we went down and met each other. (A, S&R, p. 61)

Another cautious person was Martin:

> It wasn't my natural mother who was looking for me; it was my half-sister – well, what I thought at the time were two half-sisters looking for me – but it all came out it was one full sister and one half-sister. I left it a while before I made contact with them – about 12 months – I sat back and really thought about it before I went ahead with it and wrote a letter back. I wanted a counsellor first and shortly after I got the letter I went to a counsellor and went through all the adoption papers. I'd calmed down a bit by then. I was just curious about everything. My parents were a bit upset; they weren't entirely happy with it – but they went along with it. (A, S&R, p. 51)

Others were really pleased to hear about a birth relatives' enquiry and we already know from the research that 90 per cent of all the non-searchers went on to have some form of contact with the birth relative. As Michelle describes:

> Knowing that she wanted me. Knowing that she never forgot about me. To find things about my background and who I look like, that was the main thing ... it worked out really well and we really get on. I think I am very lucky. (A, S&R, p. 142)

For the small but important minority (ten per cent) there was no wish to respond to the request. The reasons are a mixture of resenting the approach, feeling the birth parent has no rights, having no curiosity, wishing not to upset the adoptive parents, and feeling that too much is going on in their lives anyway. As Vincent put it:

→

> *I just think one family is enough … I can't see the point of going for a weekend miles away to visit a total stranger whom I'm never going to see again – just another person to send a Christmas card to. (A, S&R, p. 65)*

Almost everyone who was not expecting to hear from a birth relative felt a mixture of emotions – surprise, excitement, shock, curiosity and anxiety. There was a huge amount of concern about how their adoptive parents felt and reacted to the approach. Jessica says:

> *My parents were upset. The thing is, I think, my mum's explained it to me since then – when she adopted me it was 1963 and it was a very solemn sort of procedure. She remembers going to the court and swearing that she would 'take the baby as her own' and that was that. They believed that the natural parents wouldn't figure at all. So she was genuinely really upset by it and, I suppose, scared. She didn't know what would happen … I think both my parents felt as though they wished whoever it was would just keep their nose out of their lives and my life and just let things carry on. I did discuss at length with them and I said really, even though I knew it was upsetting them, that if I didn't do it, didn't see her, it would be something that I may regret in the future. So then they said: 'OK then, if you really feel you need to go ahead with it, you must do, and we'll try and support you with that.' (A, S&R, p. 63)*

Often the adopted person had wanted to receive their adoptive parents' blessing before they went ahead with any sort of contact. Alan, for example, added that he was only willing to meet his birth mother when he was assured that his adoptive parents were happy for him to do so:

> *The last thing I would want to do would be to upset them in any way – no way whatever. They are more to me – they've been everything to me and still are. (A, S&R, p. 62)*

And as David tells us, after receiving a letter from the adoption agency, he wanted to seek his adoptive mother's approval before he took any further action:

> *The first thing I did actually was to ring my mother to let her know because in that short space of time I realised I wanted to do it. Something inside me made me realise that I must go further with this and I told my mother and she gave me her blessing.*

Whether the adopted person went on to have contact or not, the majority felt that it was right to be informed of the enquiry. As Carol says:

> *If there was such an enquiry I think it would only be fair – yes, I think I would want to be told. I think it would be only fair that any further steps, if somebody was keen to get in touch, it ought to be the onus*

> *on me to respond – not on the agency to make a decision in the middle. I think that would be fair.*

Charlotte, too, thought it was right to be informed but also to acknowledge that, once approached, it can put the adopted person in an awkward position as it can be difficult not to take things further. She does, however, think that there should be a facility that enables adopted people to let their wish to retain their anonymity be known:

> *I think that adopted people should be aware of a birth relative's approach but they should be able to record their right to anonymity, so if a birth relative pitches up, then they have absolutely no right to approach the adopted person because they've said: 'I never want to be approached', but with the reservation that they could change their minds at any time … It's alright for people to say 'Well, you got our letter about your birth mother's approach and you could have said no,' but you can't! I'd say that I'm a very strong person but I couldn't resist it. (A, S&R, p. 60)*

What is important is that adopted people, who have not actively sought information from the adoption records or initiated a search for birth relatives, have the opportunity to think and reflect on how they want to go forward with the enquiry. Although they may have had thoughts about their birth family, they may not be so far advanced in their thinking as adopted people who are proactive. They may need more support and advice from the adoption agency before a decision is made. Some people may want to see the records first but, as we know from Mike, even the experience of gleaning background information can raise some unexpected and unsettling feelings:

> *There was an awful lot of information there that I just didn't know about; I mean quite serious information. You know, big things like my name, pictures of my mum, a letter from her … I think with hindsight it might have been better to know roughly what to expect. I didn't realise it would be as intense … but it was information that I felt I deserved as a human being. It was information that belonged to me. (A, S&R, p. 64)*

→

Questions

Show video clips of Anna, David, Carol and Jane.

☐ How can you use the research evidence to help you contact and prepare for a non-searcher's reaction on hearing that a birth relative would like contact?

☐ What are the range of responses a non-searcher may have to the enquiry?

☐ Do you think that positive reactions by non-searchers to being traced suggest that they are really people who would have searched eventually?

☐ When a birth relative decides to contact someone who has decided not to search for them, why do you think that they have not had a common interest in finding each other?

☐ How is a non-searcher who is traced by a birth relative in a different position vis à vis their adoptive parents to that of a searcher?

☐ What would you do if a sibling wants to contact the adopted person but the birth mother has expressed no desire to have contact?

Exercises – small discussion groups

Adoption professionals and counsellors

Discuss: What preparation and counselling provision do birth relatives need before an approach is made to the adopted adult? Describe the circumstances where you would make a decision not to offer the birth relative an intermediary service.

How can you prepare an adoptive parent for the possibility that a birth parent may make contact through an intermediary? How do non-searchers need to be supported in making a response that feels comfortable to them?

Adoptive parents

Discuss: Describe what your gut feelings would be if a birth parent contacted your son or daughter via an intermediary service.

Describe the circumstances when you think the adoptive parent has the right not to inform their son or daughter of a birth relative's enquiry.

○ What do you think is the motivation behind a birth parent deciding to search?

○ Would you feel differently about this

Exercises – continued

contact depending on whether the
birth parent
– relinquished voluntarily
– neglected or abused their child and
there was a contested adoption?

○ Describe the support you feel
adoptive parents need when a birth
relative has made contact via an
intermediary service.

Adopted people

Discuss: At what age do you think
adopted people should be told about a
birth relative's enquiry and desire to
have contact? Describe some of the
advantages and disadvantages of
contacting the adopted adult directly
to let them know of a birth relative's
enquiry.

5

A time of uncertainty: contact and the meeting

A TIME OF UNCERTAINTY

Introduction

Making contact and developing a relationship with a birth relative can take many forms and there can be different consequences and outcomes in the short, medium and long term. Even when the search has been successful in locating a birth parent, this does not guarantee that a meeting will take place or that a relationship will develop. Some adopted adults and birth parents might take things slowly and may exchange letters or emails for a long time before a meeting is arranged. There have been examples of an exchange of letters lasting five years before the eventual meeting. In other situations, there may be a series of conversations on the telephone. Some birth mothers feel that they cannot have contact until they have told their husband and other birth children about the adopted person; others may have contact without wanting their husband or other children to know. Others just cannot wait and meet up at the first opportunity.

Whichever path is chosen, the impact of making contact and having a reunion should not be underestimated. In this chapter we look at the different experiences adopted people have when a contact is made and a meeting takes place.

What research tells us

Eighty-eight per cent of adopted people had begun their search within six months of receiving information from their adoption records. The exception was to delay the process.

But even before they had received information from adoption records, 75 per cent of searchers said that they wanted to trace their birth mother; 40 per cent said that they would like contact with a birth brother or sister; and 38 per cent had also decided that they wanted to search for their birth father. An ambitious 11 per cent hoped to find their birth mother, father and brothers and sisters. But, in practice, once the search was underway, 91 per cent of searchers said that their birth mother was the person whom they wanted to find first. Eleven per cent of searchers thought that they would find their relative quickly. In fact, 41 per cent of those who looked for their birth mother found her within a month and 60 per cent had found her within three months. Thirty-three per cent of those looking for their birth father found him within a month, while 53 per cent had made contact within three months.

Fifty-eight per cent who made contact with their birth mother also found themselves meeting birth brothers and sisters. However, eight per cent of those who managed to trace their mother found that she had died.

First, contact with birth mothers was most likely to be by letter or telephone (91 per cent) and only nine per cent went straight for a face-to-face meeting. Most people (78 per cent) used an intermediary to establish first contact and the others (22 per cent) made contact directly themselves.

Both searchers and non-searchers were equally likely to describe the relationship with their birth relative as one of a close friendship (36 per cent searchers and 54 per cent non-searchers). Searchers were, however, more likely to describe feeling an instant connection and bond on their first meeting. Fifteen per cent of both searchers and non-searchers felt a distance and that the relationship was more like that with a stranger.

The contact

Anticipation of contact with a birth parent may involve a variety of emotions: expectation, excitement, anxiety, fear of disappointment, hope of a new relationship, curiosity. No one knows what will happen when that first contact is made or what the long-term outcome will be. Heather describes the enormous emotion she felt simply waiting for a reply to the letter sent to her mother:

> So I was braced for a good many weeks [to wait]. As it was, it was only 24 hours. But during that 24 hours I managed to cry my way through boxes of tissues, be physically ill – shake, shiver, sweat and carry on – I had no idea how long ... if this had gone on for weeks there would have been nothing left for them to have found.

We have already seen (p. 33) how Heather needed reassurance by having her mother's telephone message played back several times.

Andrew, too, has said how he experienced great feelings of excitement before he met his mother at the age of 24:

> I couldn't believe I was going to meet someone with whom I had a genetic link.

He felt an immediate emotional bond which proved to be mutual.

The meeting

Some people do not want a physical meeting – the adopted person may just want to let the birth mother know, perhaps through an intermediary, that they are well and happy. Equally, the birth mother may want the child to know that she is alive and willing to communicate any information that may be requested but may not feel able to meet.

→

When a meeting does take place, however, it can be as varied as the people involved. They can run the whole gamut of the emotions: meeting a friend, finding someone who is easy to get along with, experiencing an instant family connection, being emotionally confused and feeling elated to feeling flat. But what many adopted people report is how amazed they were at the physical similarities between themselves and their birth parent.

When Nimmy met her birth father for the first time, his first words to her were, 'My God! It's like looking in the mirror'. Nimmy's reaction was equally emotional:

> To have someone who was my flesh and blood was extraordinary.

Nimmy tells what happened when she and her father reached his house:

> ... [I] took him into the bathroom and we just stood in front of the mirror and I had to compare eyes and nose and lips and teeth and cheekbones and ears and hands and I'm the female spit of him.

Adopted people (like their birth parents) will often experience excitement as well as anxiety before contact, but it is often only when contact has been made that the full implications of the journey that they have taken sinks in. They may have considered some of the feelings they may encounter but not realised the impact on the relative they are being reunited with. As Koshii said:

> When I finally saw him [her birth father] I was struck by the enormity of what I'd done because I'd actually gone over to Africa to meet him as well. I was calm but excited, I was anxious but I wasn't as emotional as he was. I wasn't ready for the emotion that he showed when he first met me.

Heather felt a mixture of 'anxiety, apprehension, fear and terror'. But her meeting was 'far more than I ever dared to imagine'. She said that the first words her birth mother said to her, as she met her at her garden gate, were: 'Oh, yes, you're one of mine'. She says that when she stepped out of her car the verge of grass before her mother's gate 'felt like it took ten minutes to cross'.

Beth also describes how she felt when she first saw a photo of her birth mother and the subsequent meeting she had with her:

> First of all I had a letter from her and a picture. And I remember opening this letter and looking at this picture and my husband said: 'What's the matter?' And I said: 'You don't know? You take for granted that you know who you look like ... you cannot believe what this is like.' And that's the thing that sticks in my mind. I found who I looked like and I'd gone 30 years not knowing and all of a sudden ... and when I met her, I couldn't believe that I could look like somebody else ... there was a lot more depth to this than I realised at the time. So I do remember looking – and I remember the voice, and the

mannerisms – it was weird ... She certainly didn't feel like mummy, but the bond was instant. It was there, especially when somebody looks so much like you. That's the thing I probably latched on to the most: 'I looked like somebody.' A few weeks later I met the other children. As the afternoon wore on we went for a picnic ... we could make each other laugh, we had so much in common and I thought: 'I've come home – these are my people.' I felt a closeness there that I'd never felt with my younger brother. For the first time I didn't feel different any more. (A, S&R, pp. 116–117)

Jessica had a similar experience to Beth:

We met up in a restaurant in Manchester – and that was very, very emotional, very charged emotionally. I remember being totally, totally dumbfounded. Both myself and my natural mother were at first ... we both cried and both gave each other a big hug and we both spent a lot of time just staring at one another. I think we were both amazed at the similarity of our physical appearance ... it all just seemed so natural ... we were in this restaurant and it closed about three o'clock but the waiter realised there was some sort of reunion going on and he said: 'Carry on and we'll clear up around you.' And we were there until about eight o'clock that evening when the next setting of people came in to eat. Time just flew! I can't really remember what we talked about now! (A, S&R, p. 120)

Even though meeting a birth parent can be immensely satisfying, it can also be very nerve-racking as Mike describes:

I mean, obviously, it was a difficult day. It's more nerve-racking really. Twenty-eight years of not knowing who she is and thinking about it ... and it's the same for her, I mean she was nervous. I think we gave each other a hug and then we went

lives | David

David was adopted in August 1956 at the age of two months. He is the eldest of four adopted children (two boys and two girls), all from different birth mothers, and all of whom were adopted at under one year of age between 1959 and 1964. His adoptive parents then went on to have their own child, a girl who was born in 1967. David thought he would never embark on a search for his birth family, but in August 1997 his birth mother made contact with him through an intermediary. He has gone on to develop a close relationship with her and they are in regular contact. David works as a stores assistant at a government establishment. David has been married since 1993 but they have no children and his wife was always aware of him being adopted.

He speaks about his experience as a non-searcher who has embraced the contact his birth mother initiated.

> *down to the pub after about half an hour and it was fine. We got on well immediately. Difficult day though. (A, S&R, p. 118)*

Meetings can also be painful: they can bring to the surface so much about the past and the thoughts of the intervening years. As Sally, a searcher, said:

> *I felt a bit nervous, but I didn't get 'Oh, my baby' or anything like that. I mean neither of us were – or ever have been – emotional with one another ... I think I felt a slight bit of disappointment that she's just like any other working-class woman and she's not, you know, somebody special! Which I think, you know, I would have liked really ... We got on well as you would meeting somebody socially and you could manage to spend a couple of hours with them. There was no, like, antagonism between us but it wasn't, like, this big connection, and there never has been really. (A, S&R, p. 117)*

Many people meet a few times and curiosity is satisfied on both sides; for others it is the beginning of a friendship. But in Helen's case, although the first meeting was a happy one and she shared many similarities with her birth mother, their relationship did not continue:

> *We met outside the front door. It was a very, very emotional moment. We just kept looking at each other. It was really, really strange. It was like a magnet. I just kept looking at her and I suppose she just kept looking at me, noticing things. I noticed straight away that we had exactly the same eye colour. I felt very close. It's hard to describe the feeling. The only closest thing is when you're in love with somebody. It's that sort of intense feeling and closeness. We met up again, fairly soon after and I said, 'Perhaps we could meet one evening?' But she cancelled it and that was it. It was obvious from the second meeting that we weren't going to be, you know, like people who get reunited and are always seeing each other. I didn't really want that. I always knew I didn't want a replacement family, so I wasn't looking for that but I had hoped we'd see each other more often. So that's been a bit of a disappointment. I know where I come from genetically. I've met her. The mystery has gone. The gains are the missing pieces, if you like, being put into place. And I suppose I do feel a loss insofar as I've contacted her and now I've lost her again. It's better to do it because otherwise you'll always wonder, even though there are difficulties to me now – the rejection – I'm still glad I did it, because otherwise it's such a question-mark over your life. Overall, definitely it's been worth it. (A, S&R, pp. 121–122)*

Or Arnold who met his half-brother but did not like what he found and decided not to be in touch again:

> *My birth mother had died three years previously and I'd found my half-brother who had also been adopted ... I took the bull by the*

horns and arranged to meet him at his home. I was terribly nervous before the meeting … I took flowers for his wife and I also took a complete copy of my research for him … I think it's true to say I'd gone there with trepidation, not really certain what I was doing. And when he opened the door … I didn't actually take to him, and he also had a black eye. He'd gone down to a local pub with his son a few days earlier and had a fight with him.
(A, S&R, pp. 120–121)

As we have already mentioned, relationships that develop after the first meeting can take many forms. Sometimes it is a very smooth transition from stranger to friend to family, but other relationships can face many challenges before they get it right. This is Estelle's experience:

It's been a roller-coaster with my natural mother! 1994, we got on really well. 1995, she was just trying to steer me away from my family, the one that I'd always been with, and I suddenly found myself feeling very loyal to them, sort of … I suddenly realised that she was just waltzing into my life and acting as if she's given me everything, but they were the ones who'd put me through university and everything. So I was backing them up and then she felt as if she was made to feel rejected and so she went back to St Lucia and wrote me a very hostile letter and then we exchanged hostile letters for a long time. And then in 1996 we were barely in contact at all. And this year, it's been the best year. It's almost as if we had to go through that phase to work out who we were and what boundaries we can't cross and things like that, and she's made me realise that I do want to have a friendship with her.
(A, S&R, p. 123)

In the case of Sarah it was important for her that her birth mother had a realistic understanding and expectations of the type of relationship that could be developed:

I didn't cry a bit. I suppose I prepared myself a long time before – I'd done all my crying years ago ... Vera wanted to be my mother again. I had to sit down and explain: 'I have a mother'. And she was sorry she couldn't be there when I got married; she couldn't be there when I had my first two children; and shared experiences that she wanted to share with me but that's all in the past and we can't form a relationship in that. I'd rather be good friends ... She couldn't take the place of my adoptive mother just like that. I said to her: 'That's not what I'm looking for.' (A, S&R, p. 116)

Or Jemma:

Well, after the first meeting we got on quite well, even though I didn't really speak to her – the whole situation was kind of ... because we'd wanted it for such a long time ... it was nice I suppose ... I was quite excited, I was quite positive about it, we all were. She actually came back to the town where we lived ... and we just met and I kept looking at her and I saw that I had her legs and I had her hands, and we asked some questions that we wanted answered, and we got a bit of the background and that was all good. And at that time I saw something coming out of it – even though I still found it difficult. Then after that, I invited her to stay with me, I think it was two months later, for a few days.

I suppose, because I was the only one with her, I had to talk to her and that's when everything really changed I suppose. She talked about what she'd been through – and she was basically just full of negativity – I found it really hard. I couldn't talk to her because every time I tried to talk about myself she just changed the subject and wanted to talk about herself. And she just wouldn't leave me alone. It was getting to me and I just needed a bit of space but she just wouldn't allow me to be by myself. She really didn't want to know about me or how I felt about ... how everything made me feel ... you know, about my childhood experiences, anything like that. All she wanted to do was make me really negative about life. (A, S&R, pp. 122–123)

Questions

Show the video clips of Heather, Koshii, Anna, Nimmy, Andrew and David.

☐ What sorts of things need to be considered when arranging a meeting?

☐ What are the arguments for telling and not telling adoptive parents about the reunion with birth relatives?

☐ Why and how is it natural for an adoptive parent to feel hurt or distressed when their adopted child is making contact with their birth relative?

☐ How do you explain that some adopted people feel an immediate bond with their birth parents, but some do not?

☐ Why would someone want to make initial contact by letter or telephone rather than by face-to-face meeting?

Exercises

Discussion groups

Adoption professionals and counsellors

Discuss: How can adopted people and their birth relative(s) best be prepared, emotionally and practically, for the first meeting? What feelings should they look out for and what should they bring with them? How and where is the best place to meet?

Birth parents or adoptive parents

Discuss: What would your gut feelings be about the reunion if the adopted adult

○ felt very similar to the birth family member

○ had no sense of connection with the birth family

Adopted people

Discuss: How would you expect an adopted person's relationship to change with their adoptive parents after the search had started or been completed? What do you think are the main issues that need to be considered with the adopted person, birth and adoptive relatives about contacting and developing relationships with birth relatives?

6

"You're not my daughter": rejection and the fear of rejection

Introduction

Many adopted adults are likely to be concerned about the possibility of rejection when they start their search. Sometimes even the thought of receiving a negative response from a birth parent is enough to prevent a search for a birth parent. Even when they know that their birth mother loved them but had no choice but to give them up, some adopted people believe that they were rejected because they were not good enough to be kept. Logically, they may understand their birth mother's predicament but they may find it emotionally difficult to accept. We know from *Adoption, Search and Reunion* that one of the reasons non-searchers (and also information seekers) did not embark on the search for birth relatives was because they feared rejection.

Before they make contact, most people will have some understanding of why their birth mother parted with them for adoption. They may understand that in the past being an unmarried mother was a social stigma and something to be frowned upon. However, even though they have understanding and compassion for their birth mother, they may still experience their adoption as a rejection. Hence, if an adopted person is rejected by their birth parent, when they attempt to make contact as an adult, this will be especially poignant.

So fearing rejection is not uncommon, but how does it actually feel when this happens? This chapter looks at the thoughts and feelings of adopted people who either experienced a negative response on contacting their birth relative or were rejected after the reunion relationship had begun.

What research tells us

While rejection is a common fear among adopted people, only seven per cent of those who contacted a birth parent experienced outright rejection. These people, indeed, felt like they were being rejected for a second time and they describe disappointment, frustration and hurt. But five per cent of searchers (15) were rejected by one birth parent and accepted by the other. In general, the personal characteristics and experiences of adoption of this group did not differ from the generality of those who contact birth parents and those who were rejected by their birth parents. Seventy-four per cent said that they found it hard to cope with the intense feelings which were provoked by rejection. Nine per cent (24) of the 274 searchers found their birth parent and made contact only to have it terminated within a year, often after one or two visits.

Reasons for rejection

There are a variety of reasons why birth relatives do not want to have contact. Some birth mothers may feel that the decision they made many years ago should not be altered and, therefore, do not want to have contact now. There are a few birth mothers who reject outright and some who say that they have not regretted their decision to place their child for adoption. Of birth mothers who reject, there is an extremely small number who say that they have never had maternal feelings towards their child and, of these, a few have managed to put the event behind them. Some just cannot manage reliving the painful feelings they experienced when they parted with their child for adoption. In rare occasions, a rejection may occur if the child had been conceived as a direct result of rape or an incestuous relationship.

For the majority, it is more likely to be connected with their feelings and fears about their current circumstances. For example, the birth mother (for it will usually be the mother in the first instance) may now be married with a partner and children who may know nothing of the child who was adopted. While the adopted child may not have been put out of the birth mother's mind, for all practical purposes it is a secret not to be shared with anybody.

Nimmy's initial search for her mother brought a negative response. Her mother wrote to say:

> As far as I am concerned, she's not my daughter.

She did not want further contact. She also said that she had believed that Nimmy would be adopted into a happy family and hoped and trusted that she had been. But her birth mother's rejection was 'a shock and not a shock', she says, as she had prepared herself for this possibility and it helped her that she had a strong sense of self. She said:

> I didn't feel I was rejected – just that she [her birth mother] was expressing her desire against my desire.

Subsequently, Nimmy searched and found her birth father who welcomed contact. Nimmy says that, even though her mother refused to have contact with her, the search meant that she found out a lot about herself and her birth family – for example, she discovered that she has two half-brothers and two half-sisters.

Nimmy gave what may be a common explanation of her birth mother's rejection. She thought (in the absence of being able to meet her mother to learn otherwise) that she was placed for adoption partly because illegitimacy was unacceptable but also because she was the result of a mixed-race relationship. The birth of a child in this relationship was 'a closely kept secret', and to break this would disrupt her mother's relationships with her current family, she says.

→

Coping with rejection

Being rejected is not easy to cope with, as Oliver describes. He learnt that his birth parents were married and that he had a full brother and sister:

> It was horrible, it was the most horrible thing I could ever have experienced. It absolutely wrecked me. I just went to pieces for about four days. I just didn't leave the house. I just sat in and could not, could not understand it. Twenty-three years of thinking about, you know, a large proportion of my life thought [sic] was given over to it. I was just thinking the other day actually, even the smallest, tiniest little things would spark something off, you know, I'd see someone and think, 'Do I look like that?' You know, 'Is that her, is that him?' And all the time it's there, it was there in my mind, my whole life, and when I got this call back I just, I was so not expecting it because I thought, 'Right, they're together, what is the problem?' (A, S&R, p. 109)

Claire, too, refers to both pain and bemusement at her birth mother refusing contact:

> I could acknowledge it was difficult for her [birth mother], that she had two other children, that maybe her husband made it difficult as well; I could acknowledge that she probably had a really hard time of it because I assume that she went back to her parents and carried on her life as if nothing had happened. But I couldn't understand how you couldn't want to see or know, especially after having my children. I couldn't understand this … when the opportunity was there for her not to take it. (A, S&R, p. 109)

Adopted people experience a range of feelings following a rejection. Not surprisingly, they may initially feel upset and angry and in time these feelings may change to feelings of frustration, disappointment and dissatisfaction, even if the majority had no regrets about making contact. As Sandra put it:

> I thought, 'Well, sod you, it's your loss, not mine' and I still believe it is. At the end of the day I've got my children, she hasn't got hers and that's her choice. I don't worry about things I can't change and I can't change her attitude, I can't change her feelings so there's no point. No point getting yourself all worked up about it, getting upset, getting stressed about something that I can do nothing about … I think you've got to be positive, me sitting here getting all depressed and moping about it is not going to change anything. I'm going to be the one suffering then, not her. So, in actual fact, although you might say it's a bad experience, it's brought reality home in that you don't think any more, you don't wonder any more because you know. (A, S&R, p. 110)

Tony is another searcher who met his birth mother's refusal stoically. He says:

No, no regrets. It was hard work emotionally while it was going on, it was certainly hard work when the rejection came again … I don't regret it, if anything, it's filled a lot of blanks for me and I know a lot more about me. Because I'm quite positive by nature and anything that happens in my life is pretty much down to me, I make things happen because I've had to. You want to believe, right until you get the final kick in the nose, that something will come of it. My rationale is that I went as far as was acceptable to go, without causing more upset. A long time ago I learnt to handle it, it's put away and that's it. (A, S&R, p. 110)

But if the fear of being rejected determined whether or not a search was undertaken, far fewer people might embark on that journey. But this doesn't happen for, as Nimmy, who was rejected by her birth mother, said:

I don't think the potential for rejection is a good enough reason for not tracing … the thing is to build up the sense of self.

But few things are ever wasted and as Nimmy says:

Both the embracing [by her father] and the rejection [by her mother] have been incredibly enriching for my life and if I had the chance to do it all over again I would do it the same way … for a moment I felt slightly foolish that I had set myself up for a second rejection, but I've gained so much in learning about myself as a result of it that I wouldn't change it.

And yet, Nimmy says it will not be until she has met the mother who has rejected her or had a personal letter from her that

I will find some kind of conclusion.

Rejection after reunion

Sometimes adopted people appear to have a happy and

lives | Nimmy

Nimmy is of mixed parentage. She was adopted at five months into a white, well-known aristocratic family and was one of five children. Her adoptive parents have three birth children and two adopted children.

Nimmy began her search for further information in October 1989. She located her birth father in January 1990 and continues to be in regular contact with him. She also made contact with her birth mother, via an intermediary, in 1989/ 1990. However, her birth mother refused to have any contact with Nimmy. Nimmy works as an actress and is now the mother of two children.

Nimmy speaks about the positive contact she has with her birth father and how it has felt having her birth mother deny contact and communication. She also talks about the gains and losses of the search and reunion process.

→

successful reunion with the birth parent or other birth family members but then things go wrong and contact is terminated. This can be very difficult to cope with. Petra states:

> I wish that she had thought the process of contact through more clearly and had refused it at the start rather than starting it and suddenly ending it. I felt rejected – something I had not ironically felt before as regards to my adoption. (A, S&R, p. 112)

Chloe gives her experience:

> My brother Tom decided, after years of searching for me, that I wasn't the little girl he had seen at three to four years old. I might add he had been searching for me for about 15 years. Contact stopped after three months. (A, S&R, p. 112)

When no explanations are offered, it can leave the adopted person feeling particularly hurt and confused. Fran said of her experience:

> The experience has left me feeling hurt, confused and a little resentful – no explanations were offered for her apparent change of heart. I feel my self-esteem has suffered.

Nadine felt the same way:

> I feel a complete rejection would be easier to cope with than being ignored.

Sibling rivalry and rejection

Some adopted people start their search in the hope that they may find that they have birth brothers and sisters. However, while finding that this is the case can be fulfilling, it can also provoke rejection and jealousy on the part of those whom they find. These newly found other children may feel less "special" because they are no longer the oldest child or the youngest child or the only child. A birth mother accepting her child does not mean that the adopted person's birth brothers and sisters will do the same and vice versa. There have been situations where a birth mother has named her second child with the same name as the one relinquished for adoption. This could be her way of acknowledging how special that first child was but the adopted person could see it as them being easily replaced by the second child, while the second child may feel that they were a replacement for the first one.

But whenever rejection happens, it may also come because of a feeling about a lost past, the denied opportunity for the mother to have raised the child as her own. And whatever the gains, a kind of incompleteness can often remain – this is a feeling which may be shared by many adopted people who take the momentous step to search and then find that they are rejected by the one person whom they wanted to meet.

Questions

Show video clip of Nimmy talking about her experience of rejection.

☐ Think of three reasons why a birth parent may not want to have contact with a birth child.

☐ Might there be different reasons why a birth mother and a birth father would reject?

☐ Why might birth brothers and sisters reject their adopted brother or sister?

☐ What sorts of things does an adopted adult need to hear and know about to help them prepare for the possibility of a negative response from their birth relative?

☐ How can there be a satisfactory outcome to a search if there is no meeting?

☐ Even if the adopted person is rejected by a birth parent, there may be gains. Can you think of any other than those mentioned by Nimmy?

☐ Would it be better not to have searched if the outcome is rejection?

☐ Why is it that some reunions which seem to have gone well cease suddenly after a short while? What factors contribute to this?

Exercises

Small discussion groups

Adoption professionals and counsellors

Describe the ways in which you can support an adopted person who has received what they perceive as a second rejection from the birth mother. How are they likely to feel and how can you help them manage the feelings that may be generated as a consequence of this rejection?

Adopted people

Discuss: Even when adopted people have had a negative response from a birth relative they often say that they are still glad that they have searched. Why do you think this is and what are the positive gains?

Adoptive parents and birth parents

Discuss: How do you think adopted people can be helped to understand why some birth relatives have no interest in the adopted person and do not want contact? What can be offered to help soften the blow?

"Love is great but it's not everything": people who have been adopted transracially

Introduction

Black people and those from minority ethnic backgrounds who have been adopted by a white family share many of the same thoughts and experiences as white adopted adults brought up in white families. Their adoption may have been happy or unhappy; they will have similar motives both for searching and not searching; when they make contact with their birth relatives the reactions may be the same; and they may develop and retain or not develop or retain a continuing relationship with them. But transracial adoption does add an extra dimension to the adopted person's experience of adoption and the search and reunion process.

Over the past few decades there has been much debate about the rights and wrongs of "same-race" placements. In this chapter we consider some of the particular issues that adopted adults have reported facing as a result of being brought up in a transracial family.

The National Adoption Standards for England acknowledge that children should be entitled to grow up as part of a loving family which can meet their needs during childhood and beyond. One of the values states that 'Children's ethnic origin, cultural background, religion and language will be fully recognised and positively valued and promoted when decisions are made.' Today approximately 300 children are adopted from overseas. Many of these children will therefore grow up in families with a different ethnic and cultural background from their own and therefore the knowledge we have gained over the years about transracial adoption may be particularly relevant.

What research tells us

Adoption, Search and Reunion included the experiences of 32 adopted people who had been placed transracially. Research shows that these adopted people face additional challenges. Not surprisingly, they are more likely to have felt different from their families when growing up. Seventy-one per cent of them said that they felt different compared to 48 per cent of white adopted people in white families. Transracially adopted people were more likely to begin the search for information and reunion earlier than their white counterparts (25.8 years against 31.2 years). However, when they made contact, 28 per cent (as opposed to 52 per cent of those in same-race placements) said that their birth relative was 'just like' them and 23 per cent, against 54 per cent, said that they felt 'at home' with birth relatives. Thus, 44 per cent of them, after a reunion, said that they felt 'more complete as a person', whereas this was reported by 63 per cent of those who were adopted by parents of the same ethnic background.

However, both groups reported themselves to be highly satisfied with the outcome of their efforts to search and seek a reunion, although people in "same-race" placements were more highly satisfied (72 per cent against 60 per cent).

The experience of a transracial placement

Transracially adopted people describe both good and happy adoption experiences. Danny, a searcher, said:

> I felt I totally belonged. I mean from what my mother says to me now, for the first six months I was very, very quiet and I'd just sit in the corner and do what I wanted to do by myself, but after that I was totally integrated with the family ... My extended family accepted me fully ... Yeah, I couldn't have been luckier, I couldn't have been. (A, S&R, p. 149)

Some, however, had significant questions about their sense of identity, belonging and sameness as their adoptive family. Melanie, another searcher, said:

> Most of the time I felt I belonged and other times I felt quite clearly that I wasn't part of the family. Physically, definitely physically. When I was younger it was just mainly the physical differences where I didn't feel I belonged because my interests were different, my capabilities very different. I was singing and dancing and doing all those kinds of things. My family, they were very white, blue-eyed, very pinky. [I am] overweight a little bit – and what I can do is nothing that any of them can do. (A, S&R, p. 149)

What adopted people have said is that it is important for people to grow up in an environment where they are not continuously aware of their difference. Heather said:

> I think if I had been brought up in an area with black people or the schools were mixed or something like that ... I truly think that would have helped. Just to know that you walk down the street and you might bump into somebody that was the same colour as you. I could go for flipping weeks in the area my mum lived and not see any other black people. And I think it's important for the parents that are going to adopt these children to have the knowledge, an understanding, you know. Love is great but it's not everything. It really isn't everything because I had all the love I could possibly ask for but I'm not alright. (A, S&R, p. 148)

Craig talked about similar experiences:

→

One of the things, also, to be aware of for people who want to adopt children is an awareness of where they are based geographically. I was in a predominantly white area and obviously was an ethnic minority in that area, but when I came to London, eventually, as a young adult, I'm not perceived as an ethnic minority in London. So maybe when I was brought up in the 70s I wouldn't have had the prejudice and the racism that I had in the North of England – so it's something that people need to think about when they're adopting a child with ethnicity in them.

The need for a stronger sense of identity is a common theme that runs through adopted people whether or not they have been transracially adopted. But the intensity of the issue was likely to be more pronounced with people who were black in a white family. These issues were less likely to be resolved, too, for such people. This is reflected in the fact that transracially adopted people begin their search at an earlier age. Matters of identity and belonging do seem more difficult for many of those who had been placed transracially. Although their reunion was described in most cases as a positive and satisfactory experience, it was less likely to resolve many of the issues concerning identity and belonging.

However, for others like Koshii, reunion did provide her with a much stronger sense of who she is. She talks about how, in growing up, she was unable to see where her traits, mannerisms and appearance came from. She acknowledges that her adoptive mother had always supported her but her adoptive mother acknowledged that she could not give Koshii and her adoptive brother 'the identity that we needed'. Finding out about her origins and meeting her birth father gave her a stronger relationship with her family and friends and strengthened her feelings about herself. When she met her birth father, it was a double affirmation: for herself as a person but also culturally. Koshii said:

It felt like coming home when I first met him.

And Nimmy, too, concurs:

So, in terms of my physical and my emotional identity it was fantastic to meet my father because I came to understand about myself and I gained a great deal of self-esteem from discovering that I was slightly too small even, to be attractive to people in Africa … he gave me a lot more confidence because of that cultural attitude and I learnt a lot more about myself through hearing about my African family and so on and emotionally, as I say, I understand myself a lot more – we are very similar, which can be extremely annoying.

The experience of racism

Today, there is a much stronger awareness of the importance of racial and cultural heritage in forming a sense of identity and self-esteem. Adopted people who are

lives | Craig

black, from minority ethnic backgrounds or who are of mixed heritage may have grown up in a white family and in white areas. They may have been the only black person in their neighbourhood or town. They may have suffered from racial abuse or racial discrimination. Because of this, their sense of "difference" from their adopted family may well have been greater than the sense of difference which many adopted people feel when they know that they are adopted. While Craig, who lived in an all-white area with a white adoptive family, said that he was 'smothered with love and care and attention', there was:

> the outside world where I was subject to all this prejudice and racism which gave me very, very low self-esteem and made me feel very insecure and not being able to address that with them [his adoptive parents].

Koshii was adopted by a white couple who had another adopted child, who was also black. Koshii says her sense of herself as a black person was partly enhanced by the popularity of black music when she was a teenager, as well as the fashion for Afro hairstyles. But when she was younger she experienced name-calling and racism:

> I can't say that I was aware of feeling different around that time [when she was adopted at four] but I certainly knew that I looked more like my brother than I did my parents and I certainly knew I was treated very different outside our home – the looks and the names, most of which are fortunately not around today for my own children to hear. Sometimes [I had] to run home from school so we didn't get beaten up or verbally abused. But the worse thing probably was then having to sit next to those same people in church on a Sunday. Or even go to Sunday school with them.

The research in *Adoption, Search and Reunion* has shown that transracially adopted people experienced racism both within their extended families and within the community where they lived. Many talk about feeling isolated and completely alone. Some did not always feel it was appropriate to involve their parents. Many describe, as Craig does, that although their parents did much to

Craig was placed for adoption in 1964 when he was two years old. He is of mixed parentage – his mother was white and his father was believed to be of North African origin. Craig was adopted by a white family and has two sisters, one of whom is also adopted. He began his search for information in 1991 and found his birth mother and brother and sister a year later in 1992. The relationship has not continued. Craig has not been able to find any information about his birth father so confirmation of his ethnic background remains unknown. Craig works as a drama and play therapist helping children in war zones to come to terms with their experiences.

He describes his experience of growing up as a transracially adopted person.

→

63

support them in dealing with racism, they were not really able to appreciate what it was like to be growing up black in a white community.

Craig makes a plea to adoptive parents, teachers and other childcare workers. He believes he would have been able to cope better with the racism if the adults around him had been more aware of the particular issues he had to face:

> I'd have been able to cope better with the situation if my parents had more awareness, if my teachers had more awareness of the issues relating to being an ethnic minority in school. So just more awareness of the implications of being an ethnic minority or racism and prejudice and more knowledge about my background and just more ... psychological and social support really – I needed at the time.

Craig knows no more about his father than that he was from North Africa (possibly Morocco) and also of French descent. His mother is of Irish-Catalan extraction. He was adopted by a white couple and suffered from racism and says he was 'the ethnic minority in my area'. But he never felt that being adopted made him feel different – he felt lucky to have a loving home. He did not want to discuss this with his adoptive parents because it would 'rock the boat' by giving them, he thought, the idea that he was 'a problem child'.

When Craig came to London he expected to feel more at home, but instead he encountered other problems. He always thought that living in 'a big melting pot' would mean that he would feel at home with his "race" and identity. However, he found that he was 'swimming in the middle' because black friends could not empathise with him because he was light skinned. They could not understand how he could have suffered from racism:

> I thought, when I came to London, being in a big melting pot and being very multicultural, that as a young adult in my early 20s ... I might finally be able to talk to people about these issues of prejudice and racism, but the black community, black friends I had, couldn't understand that I was subjected to racial abuse because I have so little colour in me ... so they weren't able to have empathy or understanding with me. So I found the white community had sort of rejected me – the young white community I would say – and I also found when I came to London that I didn't really fit into the black community as well ... which also made – and still makes – me a bit disturbing trying to find my place in society.

Feeling rejected

For people who are black, of mixed heritage or from a minority ethnic background, there may appear to be a double rejection – Craig said he felt rejected by society through racism and also by having been placed for adoption. Fortunately, when he met his mother, she did not reject him. She was happy to find him well and that he had been placed in a good home. Being black or of mixed heritage may have a bearing on the reunion experience. For example, Nimmy expresses how her birth mother, who is white, may not have felt able to have contact partly because of the "race" issue:

> I think my mother rejected contact for several reasons. I'm, as you see, mixed race and I was adopted into a white family but she doesn't know that. She might presume that but I am sure the fact that I was mixed race was an issue for her and her family.

Dee relates how she felt about the fact that she had never met her white mother:

> It became more difficult and more unpleasant around puberty and wanting to know what I would look like when I was older, wondering whether I had half-brothers and sisters because she [her white birth mother] was only very young when she had me ... wondering whether she'd told them about me, suspecting that she probably didn't, suspecting there was a great deal of shame around my existence and so on. And feeling, like, wanting to trace or find out something. I used to say to friends: 'I don't want to meet her. I just want to see her walking down the end of the street so I can see what she looks like, I've seen her – flesh and blood – and she's a reality.' That just chokes me up. (A, S&R, p. 148)

→

Questions

Show video clips of Craig, Koshii and Nimmy.

☐ Compare the experiences of Koshii and Nimmy. How are they similar and how are they different?

☐ How might Craig's experience be different from that of Nimmy because, although both are of mixed ethnicity, he is light skinned?

☐ How can transracially adopted people be helped to have a sense of belonging?

☐ How can a child who is transracially adopted be helped by his or her adoptive parents to develop a sense of identity?

☐ Describe the different experiences black adopted people may encounter compared to white adopted people during the journey of the search and reunion.

☐ What are the different ways in which "race" can impact on adopted people and how might "race" affect a person's decision to search or not to search?

Exercises

Adoption counsellors and professionals

Discuss: How does the home environment, the extended family and the wider community that the child lives in enhance the child's ability to develop their racial and cultural identity? What does research tell us about the experience of adopted children who were placed in a family with a different cultural and ethnic background? How can it be used to inform our practice today and, in particular, for the families who have adopted children from abroad?

Adoptive parents

Imagine you are Craig's adoptive parents when he was between ten years of age and his early teens:

○ What could you say or do to ensure that he knows that you want him to feel able to discuss with you any bullying, name calling, or racism that he may experience?

○ What networks or support could you build up for yourself and for Craig?

○ What could you alter in your home environment to reinforce your message and strengthen his identity?

○ How could you build resilience in Craig?

Exercises continued

What are the factors that might lead a transracially adopted adult to feel

○ a stronger connection with the birth parent who reflects their black or minority ethnic origins

○ a greater distance and more discomfort?

For the white adoptive parent, what are the particular thoughts and feelings that may be expressed as a result of their son or daughter meeting with the parent who reflects their black or minority ethnic origins?

Adopted people

Discuss: How much do you agree with Koshii, Craig and Nimmy's experiences of growing up in a family and community which is culturally and racially different to their own? In your experience, how can a child who is transracially adopted be helped to develop a positive integrated identity and a sense of "belonging", while valuing their differences?

8

"I feared losing control": managing new relationships and feelings

Introduction

We know from the accounts of the adopted adults who appear in the video and who took part in the research that the journey of search and reunion for birth relatives is an emotionally challenging one. To search is to open a Pandora's box, where you can never be really sure what you will find and what effect this may have. An important part of the contents of this box is the adopted person's own feelings and he or she will have to face the task of managing them and managing the new relationships that may be made. One's own hopes and expectations may not be in tandem with those of the relative who has been found. Contact and reunion is a time for readjustment and change for all involved: the adopted person, the adoptive parents, the birth parents and their family.

In this chapter we look at how the people involved manage the new relationships and also the feelings that are generated as the new relationships do or do not develop.

What research tells us

Initially, most people felt that their relationship with their adoptive parents was unchanged by their contact with their birth relative. Sixty per cent of searchers and 64 per cent of non-searchers said this. However, 28 per cent of searchers and 26 per cent of non-searchers did say that they felt that the contact had caused some strain in their relationship with their adoptive parents. Eight per cent of searchers and six per cent of non-searchers said that this relationship had actually improved as a result of the contact.

Sixty-three per cent of searchers compared to 55 per cent of non-searchers were still in contact with their birth mother five years on after the initial reunion. Fifty-three per cent of searchers and 27 percent of non-searchers were still in touch with their birth father. Seventy per cent of searchers, compared to 50 per cent, were still in touch with a sibling five years on. Of those adopted people who were still in touch five years on, 67 per cent were having weekly contact with their adoptive mother and 24 per cent were in weekly contact with their birth mother. While there were high rates of satisfaction and positive evaluations of the search, contact and reunion process, for both searchers and non-searchers, the relationship with the adoptive parents and emotional bonds remained strong.

Non-searchers had to decide how to respond to a contact which they themselves had not initiated. In most cases they felt aware of their adoptive parents' position and feelings. They wanted to offer them their support and also wished to reassure their adoptive parents that wanting to see their birth relatives was not a threat to their relationship.

Managing new relationships

A successful search and positive response following contact may bring with it new relationships that may range from feeling more like a friendship to a close family relationship, such as father and daughter, mother and son, brother and sister. Some relationships will be short-lived but others may develop into a deep emotional bond. Andrew certainly uses the word "friendship" to describe his relationship with his birth mother. For him she could not replace the mother–son relationship he already enjoyed with his adoptive mother. When he talks about his adoptive mother he says:

> *From my adoptive mother's perspective, in the past whenever there was a sense that emotional bonds were somehow under threat, some positive reassurance could always be given that nothing would change because in my mind no matter what events took place I still only had one mother – the one who raised me.*

But he also acknowledges that a close relationship has developed with his birth mother and that she is certainly a permanent feature in his life.

Nimmy, too, regards her father as a friend although she is aware that from his perspective he would prefer to have a daughter–father relationship, which she cannot give.

Susie, another searcher, said:

> *As far as the relationship is concerned, it's me really because she [her birth mother] would have more involvement in my life. She would like to be – not mum because she knows that she would never be my mum now. She'd like more involvement, and although Wendy's my blood mother, she's not my mum. My mum is Jean because she has always been there for me. She has always picked me up when I've been down, looked after me when I've been ill. So that's what you call mum. (A, S&R, p. 138)*

Craig never wanted to kindle a mother–son relationship. His reasons for contacting his mother were pragmatic: he wanted to know why he had been "given away" and, given his racial mix, what his genetic inheritance on his father's side was. Fortunately for him, his birth mother, too, was not seeking anything more from the contact.

Brynn found that his relationship with his birth mother brought with it a sense of belonging. As he says:

→

It's nine years since I found my birth mum ... I can tell my natural mother an awful lot more than my adoptive mother, I suppose because she's more worldly wise. I can tell her anything and we have a lot in common, the way we talk, mannerisms, personality. It's actually a feeling of belonging in a way. Although I know I belong with my adoptive parents, and that will never be taken away or changed, it's still a nice feeling of belonging ... and it's laid the ghost to rest so to speak. I see both parents about equally I suppose, but I do feel connected to my natural mum, no doubt. (A, S&R, p. 52)

Managing the relationship between the adoptive and birth family

One of the challenges for adopted people who have had a successful reunion with their birth family, and where these relationships continue, is how they integrate these new relationships into their lives. Sorting out frequency of contact, who should be seen and when, or whether both families – adoptive and birth – can meet and get on may occupy the adopted person's thoughts.

Just as new people come into the successful searcher's life, that person also has to manage existing relationships with his or her adoptive family. The adoptive parents or brothers and sisters continue to be just this, but new feelings and perspectives may develop. And, of course, there may be new relationships between adoptive and birth parents. As we know from Andrew's experience, his birth mother met his adoptive parents and, indeed, his birth mother and adoptive mother went on holiday together. Andrew's story brings together a number of these aspects:

... within two weeks I had met most of her [birth mother's] family – including a half-brother and sister. I didn't tell my adoptive parents immediately – and when they were eventually told they were very upset. I did my best to reassure them that nothing had or would change between us, with varying degrees of success over the years.

Sometime later my birth mother, adoptive parents and myself had a meal together – I think this mainly came because of a desire for some sort of resolution on the part of my adoptive parents. Everything appeared to go very smoothly but there were understandably many very complicated emotions at work. The contact between my birth mother and adoptive mother continued – mainly through telephone calls and a few years ago they decided to spend a week in Italy together. I am still in awe of the courage and openness that this must have taken on both their parts and I've got no idea how they really felt that week or the details of their conversation – much as I would like to really!

I had mixed feelings. On the one hand it was a tremendous feeling of completion ... But on the other hand I had become used to having both sides separated; in fact, I feared losing control. With me always in the middle I had some control over issues and how events were presented – with them [his birth mother and adoptive parents] in direct contact there was the potential for large-scale emotional fallout that I had no control over, but would still feel some responsibility for because it was me that decided to open everything up and initiate the search. In fact, there's never been any large-scale emotional fallout but there have been quiet, emotional shifts in all of us. I no longer feel any great responsibility for them all – good or bad.

Nimmy, too, refers to 'friendship' with her father but, unlike Andrew, she avoided finding herself in the middle of 'all that emotion' when her adoptive parents met her birth father. She asked that they meet on their own, without her being present:

My mother and father met him – I asked them to do it separately from me because I could not bear the idea of being in the middle of all that emotion – and my mother was very taken with how similar the things that we do physically were ... our gestures and so on and they stayed in contact ... he's mainly initiated that. He came to my wedding and he came the day after my daughter was born and saw her and has completely and utterly embraced her and my family.

Others, too, have managed to integrate the birth family into their life with their adoptive family, as Barry describes:

My mum and birth mum first of all had a talk on the phone, and that was quite emotional, I think. I think mum was sort of thanking her for me and she was thanking mum for looking after me and bringing me up. And then the first Christmas my adoptive mum did a photo album, a selection of photographs, right from as a baby, right the way through to an adult, and gave it to her as a Christmas present, which she's still got ... and they still keep in touch. (A, S&R, p. 139)

For others the integration does not happen, as in Tina's and Beth's experiences. Beth says:

My parents met my birth mother and my half-siblings. They stayed two or three hours and that was enough. They won't ever have to meet them again, but at least when I talk about them by name, they'll know who they are ... they got on fine but I don't think it would be a good idea to try to make them friends. They've only got one thing in common at the end of the day and that's me. (A, S&R, p. 139)

Tina says:

As for my adoptive mother, she's been completely hopeless about the whole thing: 'I don't want to know about that bloody woman. Why should I know about her, what's she ever done for you? Don't ever mention her name to me again.' And she's never asked about her.

She's never wanted to see a photo of her and assumes that because she's blotted it out of her mind therefore I can't be seeing her again. As far as she's concerned, it's a selfish thing: 'She gave you to me; she can't come back on the scene now.' I have such an appalling relationship with my adoptive mother anyway, it doesn't really matter … I probably feel closer to my natural mother than I do my mother because three years of therapy and three years of Prozac and my bloody awful childhood has made me realise that, you know, I've got no relationship with my mother. (A, S&R, p. 138)

Managing difficult feelings

The experience of searching for and meeting birth relatives has been described as 'being on an emotional rollercoaster'. The meeting and reunion may have been a happy experience, with both parties wanting an ongoing relationship to develop. But sometimes unexpected feelings and thoughts may crop up and the adopted person finds that they have to manage negative emotions and difficult feelings.

Andrew, as we know, was happily reunited with his mother and in the ten years since they met they have had a happy and strong relationship. Nevertheless, he was taken by surprise by suddenly experiencing feelings of rejection and anger when he became a father for the first time:

I'd always been surprised that I could not find any anger towards my birth mother stemming from some sense of rejection and, in fact, I felt this for the first time – or at least became aware of it for the first time – about two years ago. I think this was prompted by the birth of my first child and it took me a while to realise that I'd started to feel this anger when my son became the same age that I was at the time that I was given up for adoption.

Becoming a parent can generate a range of feelings, from compassion to disbelief that a mother could part with her baby. Heather, who had a happy reunion with her birth mother, describes becoming a mother herself:

And I looked down at my own daughter, who at that time was six months old, which was the same age I was when given up for adoption, and it suddenly dawned on me that they would have to drag her over my dead body before I would part with my daughter.
*   And, again, it further dawned on me that if I was half a human being – genetically or otherwise – that I pretty much owed her that she was going to be vaguely similar to me and if I would have such a desperate resistance to losing my child, or the prospect of it, then how much more so for her [her birth mother] who had actually been through it.*

While Nimmy has spoken about the effect on her of becoming a mother, she knew about her mother's background and the situation that could have caused her to place Nimmy for adoption:

> *I marvel that a woman can carry a child for nine months and let it go.*

Another common reaction, to which Nimmy refers, is when she says that her adoptive mother, in particular, and her adoptive father to a degree, felt initially threatened by the whole idea of her seeking contact with birth parents. However, Nimmy described how she had to manage her adoptive mother's anger when she found out that Nimmy had been rejected by her birth mother. She felt upset with the agency in allowing contact to have been made. Nimmy describes her reactions to this experience:

> *Anger, anger right at the beginning. I was angry with myself for putting myself up for a further rejection. I was angry with her [her birth mother] in a way I was putting my adoptive family through the experience and I felt a bit bad at the way that my adoptive mother – mum – was really upset that I'd been rejected again. So there was a lot of anger.*

Adopted people often describe how they feel they are constantly doing a juggling act trying to manage other people's feelings, sometimes to the detriment of their own. It is not easy managing feelings of disloyalty and guilt when also having to face an adoptive parent's visible upset.

Sometimes adopted people are afraid to ask questions in case the birth mother becomes upset and distressed, particularly if it is about the birth father who the birth mother would prefer not to discuss. David highlights this:

> *With regard to my birth father this is slightly difficult. I obviously don't know where he is – I knew the area he came from at the time when my birth mother knew him. He would be quite elderly now – because he was older than her. It always upset her husband, Peter, to know about him – it does cause him problems – if his name's even mentioned. Now naturally I have an inquisitiveness about this but the reception I've received from everyone in the family and the way I've been treated and the way everything has gone, I could risk throwing everything away – literally, I've been warned about this – I could risk throwing everything away if I try to go after him. I do know that he did try to do the decent thing by her but wasn't able to.*

David, however, acknowledges the place that partners have in the search and reunion process. He shows real concern and sensitivity for his birth mother's husband:

> *He has been marvellous to me – he has always treated me as one of the family, from the very, very beginning. I have an unending respect for the man. He is great. He's a first-class chap.*

→

Sometimes other relationships develop or are rekindled as a result of the contact and reunion, such as in Sarah's case:

> When I first met my father two years ago, I rang my birth mother and said: 'Charles [her birth father] is here for his father's funeral. I'm meeting him next Friday for dinner – do you want to come and have dinner with us?' She arrived an hour earlier and I could tell as soon as I arrived that I wasn't needed. The spark was there and they just had eyes for each other and I sat there like a gooseberry while they reminisced about the 60s. I was a bit upset because I thought this is the last time I see my father before he goes back to South Africa [where he was then living] and why should she butt in ... neither of them were in a solid marriage so unfortunately I got them together at the "wrong" or the "right" time. So they're blissfully happy together now – she's over in Australia [to which they emigrated] and they've got a house together and it's just one big fairy tale! I speak to them both every week. Before he married my birth mother he wrote: 'For me to act as your father would be inappropriate and morally wrong but I hope that I can become a friend that loves you very much. If at any time you need a shoulder to cry on or a butt to kick I promise I will be there for you ...' Charles has always been a friend. (A, S&R, p. 125)

For some people, as in Ruth's case whose adoptive mother died, search and reunion open up deep feelings and thoughts about the losses adopted people experience and how it affects the decisions they make in their lives.

> I've got very odd thoughts about mothers and motherhood and mothering in general, because of my own experiences. It's actually a negative thought that I have because mums go away, mums leave you, mums die – even though in between I've had good experiences. But I've got to understand myself more. I've chosen at quite an early age not to be a mother ... (A, S&R, p. 130)

The problems of "genetic attraction"

Sometimes people who have been reunited, experience feelings that resemble those when people fall in love. This can feel very uncomfortable particularly if it is between an adopted person and his or her brother, sister or birth parent. This is referred to as "genetic sexual attraction". It is usual for this to be discussed during counselling so that, if it does happen, it can be recognised and steps taken to prevent such feelings getting out of hand.

Often people feel aghast at the thought that this could happen to them and that they could feel sexually attracted to a birth relative, but after meeting birth relatives they can develop a greater understanding of how such feelings can occur. When they meet their birth relatives and find they have a lot in common, share the same sense *lives* | Heather

of humour and where there is a natural affinity, it can be easier to understand how people can fall in love. When adopted people have not been brought up in the same household with their birth brothers and sisters, they have not developed the normal boundaries that brothers and sisters have. They are a stranger but one with whom they get on particularly well. Knowing that these intense feelings may occur can also help people feel more able to speak openly about them, either with another family member or an adoption counsellor.

Managing difference

Meeting birth relatives and people that look just like you can bring with it a sense of completion and a great deal of satisfaction. Nonetheless, reunions with birth family members can also highlight differences that may be the result of a different upbringing. Sometimes these differences may not affect the development of a relationship following a reunion, as in Nimmy's case, but in other cases, like Arnold's, the differences may not be overcome.

Although Nimmy learnt about her African family and gained new insights that helped her to learn more about herself, she was not able to bridge the differences between herself and her birth father. She and her black father were culturally and educationally very different – she is an adoptive daughter of a large white, aristocratic family; he was a black South African musician and actor. She said:

> The difficult thing about it is we are educationally and culturally different and so places where he expects to meet me on common ground – it just doesn't happen because my references are completely different to his – and he kind of looks up to me greatly as somebody who is extremely well educated and doesn't believe himself to be so. But we continue to investigate our relationship and try to strengthen our relationship and I would regard him as more of a friend than a father. Though my daughter ... I've given her his last name as one of her middle names, so that she has that connection with him, because I do see

Heather was adopted in 1961 at the age of eight months, and was the only child of her adoptive parents. She began her search in February 1989 when her first daughter was six months old. Her mother was located within a month and was delighted to have news of Heather, who she had always hoped would trace her family. Since their first meeting in April 1989, they have developed a very close relationship. Heather has five half-siblings whom she is also close to. Some years later she traced and met her birth father. Although they met twice and got on extremely well, they mutually agreed not to pursue the relationship other than to maintain current contact details should either one ever need to get in touch. Heather has a further eight half-siblings on her father's side but has not contacted any of them. Heather is married with two daughters and works as a part-time teacher and author.

She talks about what motivated her to search and the positive gains from developing a relationship with her birth mother and siblings.

→

> *him as her grandfather on one level. But myself, I don't consider him my father although he is in some respects as well! I don't know what that means if anything at all! It's difficult, too, because he in a sense demands a real father–daughter relationship which I'm unable to give him, but I give him a very big warm friendship.*

But for Arnold the differences were untenable when he met his birth half-brother:

> *... when he opened the door ... I didn't take to him, and he also had a black eye. He'd gone down the local pub earlier with his son and had a fight with him. With his own son! I had an instant feeling that things were not right for a ready-made new family for me. I'm not a very tactile person, strangely enough, and having rejected him personally, privately at the door, it became worse when he cuddled me when I arrived there. So we sat down ... I gathered that he'd had a very, very hard upbringing and he did not like his adoption at all. He'd not really had a settled working life at all from what I could tell and was in desperate need of care and finding something tangible in his roots, which, unfortunately, could have been me. I spent about three hours there, the longest three hours ... I just could not really imagine opening up my family existence to someone who ends up having fights with his son. It just didn't seem right to me. The circumstances were not quite conducive to a future and I felt then that the only thing to do would be to end there and not to continue. (A, S&R, p. 121)*

Sometimes meeting birth relatives can highlight the differences that exist between the adopted person and their adoptive family. Anna, a non-searcher, described how while growing up she never felt different from her adoptive family. It is only now that she has had a reunion with her birth mother that she sees how similar she is to her. As she says:

> *And, really, it is quite ironic that since I've now met my birth mother ... it's only now that I'm starting to realise quite how different I am to my adoptive family and how much like her [birth mother] I am in my personality and in my way of thinking, and I can see the personality similarities between my brothers and my adoptive parents that I don't have. So, that's been really quite a significant part of it for me.*

Managing the unknown

One eventuality that has to be faced is that sometimes the search for information about origins may remain unknown. This can be an extremely frustrating and unsettling outcome for the adopted person. This happened to Craig. He met his mother but she could tell him nothing about his father, except that he was probably of North African origin. It was, he says, 'partially good and quite a few pieces of the jigsaw had been put together' but he found not knowing 'difficult to take' which made him 'uncertain' and:

it still made me a bit unbalanced because I thought after the trace I would know everything and I could then go forward knowing concretely who I am, where I was from.

He goes on:

It was personally frustrating and disappointing – I found it difficult to cope with at the time. But also knowing that he didn't know that I existed, [that] there was no way I could trace him. It also helped to make me realise that's as far as I could go; there was no point in putting any more energy or time in trying to find someone who doesn't know I exist – it would have been very difficult. So although there were still questions there, the chapter was closed because I couldn't go any further really.

Craig explains that when he is working abroad in countries where he does not look particularly different his 'not knowing' is no longer 'a big issue'. However, when he returns to the UK where "race" is a much more prominent issue, he feels much more bothered.

Questions

Show video clips of Andrew, Anna, Sandy and David.

☐ Why do you think some people felt that the meeting with their birth mother was flat, whereas Anna (who was not a searcher) felt 'completely overwhelmed' by the experience?

☐ Why did Andrew feel like piggy in the middle once his birth mother and adoptive parents were all fully involved?

☐ Think of three questions that Andrew's adoptive mother might have asked his birth mother on their Italian holiday and three questions that his birth mother might have asked his adoptive mother.

→

Exercises

Adoption workers

Split into groups so that a different issue can be considered by three groups and then fed back.

Living with the unknown

○ Is there anything that can be done to help people live with the unknown?

○ How can their feelings be validated, and what connections can they be helped to make?

Exercise on genetic sexual attraction:

○ How can you prepare people for the possible feelings of falling in love that they may experience with their birth relative?

○ What strategies might you suggest if this seems to be happening?

Show video clip of Andrew and ask the group to identify the various feelings he had about his search and reunion and their effect on him. Then consider:

○ Can we ever prepare someone for the life-changing consequences of search and reunion?

○ Is it always possible to reach a "final resolution" of the complex emotions that can be generated?

○ How do we feel as professionals about the fact that there may be no neat solutions?

Birth and adoptive parents

Discuss: How can both the adoptive parent and birth parent have the role of grandparent when the adopted person has their own children? What anxieties and concerns do you think the birth and adoptive parents may have?

Adopted people

Discuss: Describe some of the positive and negative feelings birth parents and adoptive parents and birth and adoptive siblings may experience during the reunion and after. How can the adopted person manage other people's feelings without compromising their own?

9

Is the search ever over? The aftermath and effects of search and reunion

Introduction

Adoption, Search and Reunion makes it clear that, for many adopted adults, information from agency records and directly from the birth family can really help an adopted person gain a deeper sense of their personal identity. There are questions they can find answers to – like, for example, why do I look the way I do? or, why am I so talented at music or sport? – which people who are not adopted often take for granted. For the adopted person, answers even to these questions take on a great significance.

The search and reunion process can be a complex and challenging journey. For some it is a deeply rewarding and satisfying experience and for others emotionally draining and upsetting. It is also a journey that continues throughout life, challenging, clarifying and placing in context many aspects of life's experiences for adopted adults.

Nimmy says that her search has not finished, although her mother refused contact with her. Nimmy's is a natural and common human feeling wherever questions are left unanswered or concerns unresolved. Other people, like Craig, decide they have gone as far as they can and try to leave their questions behind them. Many other people, as we have seen, search successfully and strike up a new relationship with a birth parent – a friendship, as many commonly refer to it – and meet previously unknown birth relatives. Others meet their birth parent and find that fitting that missing piece of the jigsaw is enough. For them the journey is finished. Whatever the outcome and whatever the reaction, and whether it brings pain or joy, it is a remarkable journey, which can be the most significant that those who choose to undertake it will ever make.

In this chapter we look at what the adopted people say about that experience.

What research tells us

Whether or not contact with a birth relative was short lived, abrupt or a more long-lasting experience, for most searchers and non-searchers it was a positive one – the rates of satisfaction are different – 85 per cent for searchers and 72 per cent for non-searchers. Over 80 per cent of both groups said that contact had answered important questions about their background. Half of all the searchers and a third of all the non-searchers said that they had an improved sense of identity and well-being as a result of the contact. People referred to feeling more complete in their life story as the

→

"missing bits" are found. Twenty-seven per cent of both searchers and non-searchers said that the contact and reunion had not changed them. Sixteen per cent of searchers and non-searchers found their reunion experience to be emotionally upsetting, with nine per cent of both groups reporting that their family and social life were busier as a result.

A year after being reunited with their birth mothers, 15 per cent of searchers and ten per cent of non-searchers had ceased contact. Five years or more after the initial reunion, 53 per cent of searchers and 55 per cent of non-searchers remained in contact with their birth mothers. But 67 per cent of searchers had weekly contact with their adoptive mother, compared with 24 per cent with their birth mother.

Relationships between adopted people and their adoptive parents and siblings remained strong throughout the search and reunion process. The overwhelming majority of adopted people reported that the depth of love and affection remained unchanged. The bonds formed with their adoptive parent in early childhood are stronger than those formed in the adult years with a birth parent.

The aftermath of search and reunion

We have looked at the many responses to a successful search. Some of these – like rejection – will be painful and may have confirmed the searcher's initial fears. Most contacts end more happily – a contact which satisfies either searcher or the person sought or both. This may be one meeting (which was all that was wanted) or it may result in what is commonly seen by searchers as "friendship" and some kind of integration into the adopted person's own family life – that with their partner and children or with their adoptive family, and sometimes both. But what is known from the research is that, even when it has not ended in a way desired by the adopted person, very few still regret the experience.

As Nimmy says:

> *Both the searchings [for her birth mother and birth father] … the rejection and the embracing have been incredibly enriching for my life and if I had the chance to do it over again I would do it the same way and I have no regrets whatsoever about the fact that my mother rejected me. For a moment I felt slightly foolish that I had set myself up for a second rejection but I've gained so much in learning about myself as a result of it that I wouldn't change it.*

Or as Janet describes:

> *It is now five years on and the relationship I have with my adoptive and birth family just seems to come into its own really – there's no kind of antagonism – the only problem I do have is when it's time to visit them all – on holidays – that's the only difficulty! Because we are spread at three corners of the country – this half-term I'm going down*

on Saturday to stay with my adoptive mum and then I'm coming back on Tuesday and then on Thursday I'm up to Manchester to stay with my birth sister and that's how – to get both of them in at times ... I don't like to leave it too long between ... because it's difficult to get down for weekends and things. But there's no jostling or vying for who I'm going to visit or when. My sister is a big gain in my life which grows every day. I don't know where I would be without her now and I don't know how we managed to live without each other. (A, S&R, p. 151)

The initial interest in finding out more, as we have seen, is often about wishing to know more about who one is, where one came from, one's heritage, and knowing something as basic as who do I look like. Angela said:

It just makes you feel you belong to something because I used to very much feel as I was growing up, especially when I was going through traumatic times, like I'd just been plonked on the earth – a mystery – no past at all that you can relate to. I'd constantly think: 'Why do I think this way, surely there's something else, someone who understands about this or that?' So you feel isolated and cut off. I'm sure that's one of the reasons why wanting to find birth parents is so important because it makes you have a beginning, middle and an end. (A, S&R, pp. 140–141)

For many people it is about a resolution which may have been sought from childhood. Brynn, referring to his successful search, said:

It's a ghost laid to rest. (A, S&R, p. 129)

Andrew would agree that, like many other adopted people who have developed a relationship with a birth relative, there is a sense of completion, but he points out too that a resolution may not always be achieved. He says:

As time's progressed I have become increasingly aware that for me reunion was not an event, but a long and eventful journey that is still ongoing. There have been occasions throughout the last 11 years when I've foolishly believed that a state of resolution had been reached but something has always happened to create some sort of shift. In fact in many ways it gets more complicated ...

He goes on to say:

I would not want to give the impression that I have escaped the constant emotional changes and I'm still learning about my feelings over the adoption.

Andrew explains that, when he set out on his journey, he was not fully aware of the consequences of his action:

→

*When I decided to make contact with my birth mother I had no idea
of the scope and depth of the consequences of that action and to so
many people, and it does lead me to question whether I did the right
thing. In fact I don't think I'd have been able to stop myself but I
would have liked the benefit of hindsight in order to improve the way
I did things.*

But he sums it up by saying:

*I've certainly gained a deep sense of personal resolution from the
reunion and I know that my birth mother is overjoyed at the contact
we still have.*

Anna, who had never wanted to find her birth mother, now finds that 'she's very
much a big part of my life'.

Heather had wanted to search for some time and when she made contact, her
mother was enthusiastic to meet her. At the first meeting, her birth mother
acknowledged how similar she was and, in Heather's words, said:

*She [her birth mother] looked at me: 'Oh yes, you're one of mine-
you'll like lasagne then, come on in.' And we went in and it's gone
forwards from then on ... it's been fantastic, she is remarkably similar
to me. You add another 33 years on and you've got it ... our relatives
don't know the difference between us on the phone ... it's fantastic ...
it was far more than I'd dared to imagine and very much like some of
the others ... ten, 11 years on I still choke when I think about that
meeting over the gate.*

Nimmy's view was that:

*It was emotionally enriching ... I would not do anything differently
again.*

For Koshii, who had wanted to uncover 'the other piece of the jigsaw about my
heritage':

*... finding out about my cultural identity has given me a stronger
relationship with my family and my friends – but most of all with
myself. I now have a solid foundation from which to look back at my
past and with which to welcome the future.*

Or, as Susie says:

*Wendy's my blood mother, she's not mum. My mum is Jean, because
she's always been there for me, she's always picked me up when I've
been down, looked after me when I've been ill. So that's what you call*

a mum. Not somebody that's actually had you, given birth to you. (A, S&R, p. 138)

She also says:

Well, it's changed my personality. I'm more laid back now. I'm not so frustrated. I don't go off in a tantrum, because all the questions that were unanswered as a child and teenager and right up until my late 30s, things that have been going on in my mind, the questions that I've wanted to ask – it's all been answered now. I'm at ease; I feel more at ease within myself for knowing. My [adoptive] parents say I'm not so uptight any more! (A, S&R, p. 142)

For some adopted people the search is never quite finished or resolved. Some will come to accept that they cannot go any further, like Craig who felt that time and energy would be wasted on trying to trace a father who did not even know he existed. He had to come to terms with the fact that he would never know his father's racial identity. While for others, like Nimmy, there remain some unresolved concerns that may or may not need to be addressed in the future. She admits to 'some unfinished business' when she says:

Because it's not over … in a way it's not concluded until I've met her or had a letter from her personally or not even necessarily an explanation. But I do, in a sense, want more and so it's not over. For me the sense of it being not over is an OK feeling. I don't feel upset about it – I'm just sure that I will find some kind of conclusion.

So perhaps we can best describe the search and reunion experience for adopted people and their birth and adoptive family as similar to a stone that has been thrown into a pond. There will be an initial impact and then ripples as the impact reverberates but eventually the pond settles down.

Jane was adopted shortly after her birth in 1966. She has an older brother who was also adopted. Jane has no desire to find out any further information about her adoption or trace and make contact with any birth relatives. Jane works as a freelance journalist.

She speaks about the reasons why she does not want to begin a search for birth relatives.

→

Questions

☐ Describe five positive elements of the outcome from the search and reunion for the different parties involved.

☐ Describe five negative elements of the outcome of the search and reunion for the different parties involved.

☐ How can you enable people who have been met with rejection to come to terms with it?

☐ How might other family members (in both the adoptive and birth families) be affected by a) a successful reunion b) an unsuccessful reunion? Which family members might be more affected than others?

Exercises

Adopted people, birth and adoptive parents and adoption professionals and counsellors

Discuss: When Craig was unsuccessful in finding out anything about his birth father, he says 'the chapter is closed'.

○ How easy do you think it is to close down thoughts and feelings about someone whom you had hoped to find?

○ What difference would it have made if Craig had been given background information and accurate details about his birth father?

○ How would it have helped him to "close" the chapter?

Discuss: How might you feel if you were rejected by

○ your birth mother

○ your birth father

○ your birth sibling?

Describe what feelings would be the same and what would be different?

10

Disloyalty and guilt: adoptive parents and search and reunion

Adoptive parents will face additional challenges in bringing up a child to whom they are not genetically related and who has a second family tree.

What is clear from most people in the research and the video is that the majority of adopted people felt loved and cherished by their adoptive parents. The last thing any of the adopted people wanted was to hurt or cause distress to their adoptive parents by asking questions about the circumstances of their birth or adoption or about their birth parents or undertaking a search for them.

However, the love and care of adoptive parents cannot take away the reality of a second birth family tree or the sense of difference this can bring about. This can be particularly heightened for those children brought up in transracial placements. Like Koshii's adoptive mother, it is important for adoptive parents to recognise that they may not be able directly to meet their children's cultural needs and the need for the more complete development of a racial identity. This is an important consideration for contemporary adoptions where children may be adopted from abroad or may have been adopted by a family from a different ethnic and cultural background. For these children there will be additional tasks and challenges faced by the adoptive family if the children are to develop a strong, resilient and secure sense of who they are.

Talking through important matters related to adoption in the course of growing up as a child and then as an adult can be a difficult task. The need to think about ways of talking with the child about his or her adoption that does not make them feel disloyal or guilty is very important. But even when adoptive parents have made it clear that they have no problem about being asked questions about the adoption and birth family, there may continue to be a sense of anxiety and unease about doing so.

Adoption, Search and Reunion has shown that adopted people continue to feel close to their adoptive parents after a reunion with birth relatives, but most adoptive parents may feel anxious that their son's or daughter's search for, and reunion with, the birth relative may change the depth and closeness of their relationship. It is important that adoptive parents understand the reassuring message from *Adoption, Search and Reunion*, so that they can feel more confident and secure in their relationship and not afraid to support their son or daughter through the search and reunion process. Wherever possible, it can be important for adoptive parents to have access to networks or other sources of support where they can talk about their concerns, thoughts and feelings.

→

Questions

☐ Why do you think it is that, even when adoptive parents have a great understanding about their son's or daughter's need to search, some may still feel hurt and let down when contact with birth relatives is actively sought?

☐ What fears might an adoptive parent have about their son or daughter searching for a birth parent?

☐ How might adoptive parents feel when their son or daughter is excited by their initial contact with their birth relatives?

☐ How might an adoptive parent encourage an adopted person to be open about their inner thoughts and feelings about their need for background information and contact with birth relatives?

☐ What advice would you give to prospective adoptive parents when they are thinking about adopting a child from overseas?

Exercises

Adoptive parents, adopted people, birth parents and adoption professionals and counsellors

Discuss: An adopted person is not sure that he or she wants to search for birth family members. What sorts of things do you think adoptive parents can say that would help them reach a decision?

Discuss: What kinds of support, advice and information do adoptive parents need

○ with their child during childhood

○ during the search and reunion process?

Discuss: Why do some adopted people feel an immediate bond with their birth parents and what does this mean about their relationship with their adoptive parents?

11

A part of the circle: the place of birth relatives

A PART OF THE CIRCLE

When contact is made with a birth relative or birth parents have searched for their now adult adopted child, it is important that they have had the opportunity to think about what the contact and reunion will mean for them. Adoption counsellors have an important role in helping the birth relative think through and understand what the experience might mean.

Like all the other parties in the adoption circle, birth parents and other relatives need to feel that they have the support and advice they need to take decisions and make plans about how they may wish to respond to the adopted person's wish for contact. When it is the other way round and it is the birth mother or father or a brother or sister who wants to contact the adopted adult, through an intermediary service, it is crucial that they have an opportunity to talk thorough the implications. The benefits and disadvantages of contacting the adopted adult need to be fully considered, not only insofar as they affect the birth relative but also for the potential effect upon the adopted person and his or her family.

Sometimes a birth mother may not feel able to have contact but may be willing to let their adopted son or daughter have a photograph and the opportunity to ask some questions through an intermediary. Others may need more time to come to a decision and may want to see the adopted person but feel unable to until they have told their other children and partner about the child they had adopted.

We know that most adopted people do not harbour anger towards their birth mother about being adopted but instead talk of feelings of compassion towards her for the difficult choice she had to make. However, this may not prevent complex feelings such as joy, happiness, sadness and anger occurring when contact is made.

What seems to be important is that people make their expectations known so that misunderstandings can be prevented.

→

Questions

☐ How might a reunion with birth siblings be different to a reunion with a birth mother and birth father?

Exercises

Adopted people, adoptive parents, birth parents and adoption workers

Discuss: What would be the advantages and disadvantages of the adoptive parents and birth parents meeting for

○ the adopted person

○ the birth parents and

○ the adoptive parents?

How could you prepare them for a meeting with one another and describe the range of feelings each party may have?

Discuss: How might you help a birth mother or birth father to prepare for a meeting?

Discuss: Some birth mothers have expressed a huge sense of grief and loss following the adoption of their child.

○ How do you think these feelings of loss could impact on a subsequent reunion and relationship with the adopted person and also the adoptive family?

The critical hinge: professionals and practice

THE CRITICAL HINGE

12

The opening of adoption records has not only provided new opportunities to the adopted people who want to discover more about their origins and birth family, but it has also given adoption practitioners an insight into the world of adopted people and has enhanced our understanding of some of their thoughts and feelings. Not the least of these is what spurs them on to search or not, a discussion of which began this workbook.

Gaining a greater insight means that we have opportunities to review current practice and policy to make sure that services are appropriately provided to meet the needs of adopted people and their birth and adoptive families. All the adopted adults in the video and in this book provide poignant messages for adoption practitioners, managers and policy makers. Listening to their particular experiences can help adoption professionals, as well as others who work in the field of childcare and family relationships, to develop their learning and understanding. This can also enhance the role of the practitioner as someone who is often a critical hinge in the relationship between adopted person and birth parent.

But can we learn from these experiences in order to improve placement practice today? When children are placed for adoption now, the need to gather as much information as possible about the child's origins and family history cannot be over-emphasised. We know from the people in this workbook that not all adopted people want to search. However, for those who do, there is frustration and often pain when large parts of the adoption jigsaw are missing. These missing pieces can supply answers to questions that may have bothered the adopted person for years. Finding them can allow a sense of completeness and a strengthened personal identity.

For some this will not be easy and may even be impossible. The position of abandoned babies is one example: with these children even the most basic information can be important – what the child was wearing when found, photographs of where they were found and who the person was who found them.

Another group whose personal history may well be incomplete is children adopted from abroad. Those children may also come from countries where record-keeping is not so well established or where records are destroyed and families scattered as a result of war, civil strife and natural disaster. But there are also children who arrive as unaccompanied asylum seekers. Some of them may never be reunited with their parents or families or may never, as children at least, return to their own countries. These lessons apply for them too.

Professionals know that just as adoption does not end with an order being made,

→

neither does the one session of birth records counselling give all the necessary support and advice a person needs. Everyone is different and each experience needs to be understood for the meaning it has for the individual. This means that professionals need to work within a framework that offers a flexible, non-discriminatory service that allows adopted people and their birth and adoptive relatives to tap into services as and when needed.

Adopted people have clearly found it helpful to have the opportunity to talk about their experience of being adopted and their hopes, fears and expectations of the search and reunion process. It is important that throughout their lives they have access to the help and support they need. As Nimmy says, it is really helpful to talk about the issues that may continue for the adopted person long after the contact and reunion have taken place. This means giving adopted people the time to think about what lies behind their motivations, giving them time to reflect and offering them the opportunity to discuss their expectations.

Not every adopted person will tell their adoptive parent about their desire to find out more information about their origins or that they have indeed searched and found birth relatives. The counsellor will, of course, need to help the adopted person consider the advantages and disadvantages of this, but what is important is wherever possible to let the adoptive parent know that they, too, can seek information, counselling and advice.

It is important for professionals working in family placement today to help prepare adoptive parents for the very real possibility that their son or daughter may seek information and contact with birth relatives when they become adults. The implication of this is how they will manage the feelings that may be generated as a result of such searching. Providing support and finding ways so that adoption and the child's background can be a subject that is talked about in a comfortable and open way is a real challenge, but one that needs to be met. In contemporary adoptions it is likely that there will be a greater openness as many will retain some link with the birth family, either through a letterbox agreement or personal meeting. Whatever contact arrangements are agreed, they will need to be managed and reviewed to address changing needs and circumstances.

Questions

The following can be used for training family placement workers and also social work students including post-qualifying social workers.

Clips of the video showing the range of adopted people's experiences can be used to promote group discussions in the following areas:

☐ Why is it important to have information and a sense of connection with your birth family?

☐ Discuss how the interplay between nature *v* nurture affects the development of a child's sense of identity, their feeling valued and that they belong.

☐ When recruiting and selecting adoptive and foster parents, how can you help them prepare for the task of parenting and looking after a child who is not genetically related?

☐ How can adoption professionals enable parents and children to feel more comfortable about talking about the adoption and the child's family background?

☐ Describe some of the triggers for adopted people who have decided to seek information from adoption records to begin a search for a birth relative.

Exercises

Family placement workers and social work students

Ask participants to get into pairs and talk to their partner about the name they have been given, the history behind it and what their partner has inherited from their family. How can this help them to think about the needs of children who are entering the looked after system and the importance of providing full, factual and accurate information about their family and life?

Focus on how to apply what you have learnt from the video to the kinds of tasks they undertake day to day. A case study of a child needing a permanent family placement should be given to participants. Ask the family placement

workers and students to outline how the child's long-term identity needs will be met, to include such things as type of placement, contact needs, life story work and direct work.

Discuss: When providing counselling to adopted people or people who have been in care, and who want access to information or want to embark on a search for birth relatives, how would you prepare them? What issues do you think they need to address? What support and services should be in place to assist them? Would the help and assistance that may be needed be exactly the same for adopted people and people who were fostered or brought up in residential care?

13

Making sense of who we are: the lessons of adoption for other areas of practice

Over the years we have learned a tremendous amount about how people have been affected by adoption. For instance, the importance of being open with the adopted child about his or her adoptive status and the need to provide as much information as possible so the child can grow up with a strong sense of his or her beginnings and original family history. The learning from adoption and the experience of growing up in a family with people who do not have a genetic relationship can be used in other areas where children are separated from their family of origin. In this chapter we consider some of these related areas.

When adoption was first legalised in England and Wales in 1926 and until the 1950s, it was believed that the adoption would not only sever legal ties but also the emotional ties with the family of origin. Adoption was seen as a clean break. The adopted child (then, and for a period afterwards, often a baby) became, in the minds of many professionals and adoptive parents, a clean sheet where a new personal history could be written. The child's birth and birth parentage were a kind of false start to be hidden away. The view at the time was that adoption provided a complete break with the child's origins and that the child would grow up as a member of their new family with no thoughts that there would be any need or desire to know about their origins. Adoptive parents were encouraged to tell their child that he or she was adopted, but were also reassured that, if the child felt loved and wanted, he or she would have no need to think or ask questions about their birth family and background. It is clear that human beings are not made for social engineering and, for a quarter of a century, legislation throughout the UK has reflected the fact that it is not sufficient to be told that you are adopted and to leave it at that.

Angela describes a very common motivation of adopted people when she says:

> It just makes you feel that you belong to something because I used to very much feel as I was growing up, especially when I was going through traumatic times, like I'd just been plonked on the earth – a mystery – no past at all that you can relate to. I'd constantly think: 'Why do I think this way; surely there's something else, someone who understands about this or that?' So you feel isolated and cut off. I'm sure that's one of the reasons why wanting to find birth parents is so important [it is] because it makes you have a beginning, middle and end. (A, S&R, p. 140)

Experiences like these tell us how important it is for children to have as much information about their origins as they can, so that they can make sense of why they look the way they do or have different talents and personality traits from their adoptive family.

Adoption, Search and Reunion has also shown that love and affection between the adopted person and his or her parents does not, for the vast majority, falter when there is openness about adoption or where contact has been established with a birth parent or other birth relatives.

Having gleaned such valuable knowledge from one area – adoption, search and reunion – it is incumbent upon us to ensure that it is used in, and applied to other situations where children are separated from the genetic parent, such as divorce, death or reproductive technology like donor-assisted conception.

Donor-assisted conception

An estimated 18,000 children have been born in the UK following donor-assisted conception since August 1991, with approximately 2,000 born each year. But unlike adopted children, they do not at present have the same rights to information about their genetic parents. For the majority of these children it is likely that they may never be told the truth about their conception. In most situations of donor-assisted conception, usually one of the parents has a genetic relationship with the child. However, the child's birth certificate does not reflect the truth about the child's conception as it does not give the name of the donor parent but instead the name of the "social" parent as being the parent who has the genetic relationship.

There is currently much debate about whether or not it is time to acknowledge the information needs and rights of people born as a result of donor-assisted conception, so that they can have identifying information about the genetic parent who created them by donating either sperm, eggs or an embryo. While these deliberations go on, there are a few studies that report the experience of people who have either been informed of their donor-conceived status or have found out by an accidental disclosure (Turner and Coyle, 2000). As reflected by one of the people who took part in Turner and Coyle's study, even before the knowledge of their donor-conceived status, there was often a sense of always knowing that something was not quite right. This is a common reflection of such people. As Rachel, a donor-conceived person, said:

lives | Anna

Anna always knew she was adopted but had not initiated contact with the adoption agency or birth family. Instead, Anna's birth mother initiated the contact when Anna was 24 years old. Anna felt unable to cope with any meeting at the time, but four years later decided that she was ready for it. Since then, Anna and her birth mother's relationship has grown from strength to strength and they meet on a regular basis. Her adoptive parents initially felt uneasy about Anna's relationship with her birth mother, but are now more understanding and supportive.

Anna had a baby boy in 2002 and her birth mother is an active grandparent alongside her adoptive parents. She used to work as director of human resources for a large multinational company, but now works part-time for her husband's business.

Anna describes how she felt when first approached by her birth mother and how their subsequent relationship has developed in a positive way.

→

I always felt like I didn't belong with these people – I searched for evidence of my "adoption" for many years as a child. (A, S&R, p. 204)

Just like adopted people, donor-conceived people can grow up feeling very loved and wanted, but they may also feel different from their parents and other brothers and sisters in the family. But unlike adopted people, who are usually aware of their adoptive status and therefore can acknowledge the differences, such an opportunity is denied to the donor-conceived person. If the secret is maintained and the truth denied about the child's genetic origins, it may prevent the donor-conceived person from being able to make sense of themselves and the difference they may feel. Not having available important medical information too, may result in the donor-conceived person making or not making decisions that could profoundly affect their life. This was brought to light recently after a nine-year-old donor-conceived child was discovered to have a potentially fatal condition known as Opitz's Syndrome. It was subsequently learned that that his genetic father carried this inherited gene disorder. This sperm donor had fathered 43 babies from a London clinic each with a 50-50 chance of inheriting this rare disease (Rogers, 2001).

In many ways the shroud of secrecy and the practices that have developed in donor-assisted conception mirror past adoption practice. People are not able to talk openly about it, giving it a sense that it is something that is taboo and which they should be ashamed of. Perhaps the knowledge and lessons from adoption can be applied to donor-assisted conception in order that prospective parents feel more confident about being open and honest with their child. Research has shown that the relationship and feelings of love and affection do not come as a direct result of having a biological relationship. It is much more subtle than that. These bonds stem from the quality of the care-giving relationship and the parenting and support that are given over the years. Hopefully this knowledge can go some way to encourage parents of donor-conceived children to avoid the negative experiences known to adopted people when openness has not been present and "the secret" of their origins is disclosed in an inadvertent way, for instance during a family argument.

So that those born as a result of donor assistance do not suffer from the mistakes which afflicted adoption practice in times gone by, we should listen to and learn from adopted people. They (and foundlings in particular) know first hand what it is like not to have information which helps them to make sense of themselves and to have a history that connects the past, present and future.

It is important, therefore, that prospective parents of children with whom they do not share a genetic relationship should think about the information that their son or daughter might need and the negative implications that a failure to tell the truth may have. It may be that, like adoptive parents, they should have access to support and advice that they may need throughout the child's life to help them deal with the specific issues that may arise as a result of the child's donor-conceived status.

Other related areas

As mentioned in the introductory paragraph to this chapter, there are many situations where children may be separated from their biological parents and families. For example, children who are not adopted but are brought up in long-term foster care or children who have come to this country as unaccompanied asylum seekers, as well as children who are adopted from overseas.

It is, of course, not always possible to provide the child with all the information there is about his or her background as it may just not be known. But we should endeavour to discover all there is to know so that the child can feel confident and reassured that all efforts were made to give him or her the information needed to help them have a sense of who they are. Sandy's belief was that, so far as foundlings are concerned, it is important to retain all the details of where a child is found, keep the clothing and anything else, insignificant as it may seem. Where a child is an unaccompanied asylum seeker or adopted from overseas, they will need information about their ethnicity and culture. Childcare practitioners may be the first point of contact when a child enters the looked-after system and, thus, it is crucial that accurate information is gathered.

Some people may find it difficult to understand why this is important. But perhaps by putting ourselves into the shoes of Sandy or Craig we can gain a greater understanding and insight into what it is like to not have the opportunity to answer the important questions – even the insignificant questions – they have about their background and to have to live with the unease of not quite feeling complete.

The needs of Sandy and Craig are shared by everyone, adopted and not adopted, separated, for whatever reason, from birth parents and families, or not. All of us need the opportunity to make sense of who we are and need knowledge and information to do so. The difference is that most of us take for granted such knowledge and information, whereas for many other people, the quest for it provokes a life-long search.

→

Questions

☐ What are the similarities and differences between people who are adopted and those born as a result of donor-assisted conception?

☐ In what practical ways can parents of donor-conceived children be assisted in being open and truthful with their child about his or her origins?

☐ What rights to information does a child who is fostered have?

☐ How can you provide information about the range of services offered to foster children and their foster family in an accessible way?

☐ How can you ensure that an unaccompanied asylum seeker retains their personal history and identity?

Exercises

Fertility counsellors

Debate whether or not you think it is right for anonymity to be lifted, to give the donor-conceived person the opportunity to find out his or her genetic history.

○ What are the advantages and disadvantages for the donor-conceived person and his or her genetic and social parents?

○ What needs to take place in the preparation and counselling process to help parents of a donor-conceived child to parent a child who is not genetically related?

Parents of donor-conceived children

○ What is the right age to tell a child of their donor-conceived status, if at all? Give reasons for this, outlining the advantages and disadvantages of being open with the child.

○ How can parents of donor-conceived children explain the differences in a child's physical appearance, talents and personality when the nature of the child's conception remains a secret?

○ What might be the possible consequences of keeping the nature of the child's conception secret?

Foster carers

Discuss: What hinders and helps a child to develop a strong sense that they belong to the foster family?

How can foster carers encourage a sense of family membership while enabling a child to maintain his or her relationship and place in their family of origin?

References and recommended reading

References

Feast, J and Smith, J (1995) 'Openness and opportunities – review of an intermediary service for birth relatives', *Adoption & Fostering* 19:3, pp17–23

Feast, J and Smith, J (1993) 'Working on behalf of birth families – The Children's Society experience', *Adoption & Fostering* 17:2, pp33–40

Howe, D, Sawbridge, P and Hinings, D (1992) *Half a Million Women: Mothers who lose their children by adoption*, London: The Post Adoption Centre

Hughes, B and Logan, J (1973) *The Hidden Dimension*, London: Mental Health Foundation

Rogers, L (2001) 'Sperm donor children may have fatal gene', *The Sunday Times*, 23 September 2001

Turner, AJ and Coyle, A (2000) 'What does it mean to be a donor offspring? The identity experiences of adults conceived by donor insemination and implications for counselling and therapy', *Human Reproduction* 15, pp2041–2051

Winkler, RC and van Keppel, M (1984) *Relinquishing Mothers in Adoption: Their long-term adjustment*, Monograph no.3, Melbourne Institute of Family Studies

Recommended reading

There are many books published overseas, particularly in the USA, and several journal articles, both in popular magazines and academic journals. These have been excluded from the following list on the grounds that what is offered is more immediately available. However, those wanting to look further are advised to consult an academic library or the Electronic Library of Social Work, held by the Social Care Institute for Excellence, accessible on www.elsc.org.uk.

Blyth, E, Cranshaw, M and Speirs, J (1998) *Truth and the Child Ten Years on: Information exchange in donor assisted conception*, London: BASW

Clapton, G, (ed.) (2003) *Relatively Unknown: A year in the life of the ACR for Scotland*, Edinburgh: Family Care

→

Department of Health (1999) *Adoption Now: Messages from Research*, Chichester: John Wiley and Sons

Douglas, A and Philpot, T (eds) (2002) *Adoption: Changing Families: Changing Times*, London: Routledge

Feast, J and Howe, D (2002) 'Talking and telling', in Douglas, A and Philpot, T, *Adoption: Changing Families, Changing Times*, London: Routledge

Feast, J, Marwood, M, Seabrook, S and Webb, E (1998, 2nd edn) *Preparing for Reunion: The experiences from the adoption circle,* London: The Children's Society

Hodgkins, P (1991) *Birth Records Counselling: A practical guide*, London: BAAF

Holman, B (1995) *The Evacuation: A very British revolution*, Oxford: Lion Publishing

Howe, D, (1996) *Adopters on Adoption,* London: BAAF

Howe, D (1998) *Patterns of Adoption: Nature, nurture and psychosocial development,* Oxford: Blackwell Science

Howe, D and Feast, J (2000) *Adoption, Search and Reunion: The long-term experience of adopted adults*, London: The Children's Society and republished by BAAF (2003)

McMillan, R and Irving, G (1994) *Heart of Reunion: Some experiences of reunion in Scotland*, Barkingside: Barnardo's

Mullender, A and Kearn, S (1997) *I'm Here Waiting: Birth relatives' views on Part II of the Adoption Contact Register for England and Wales*, London: BAAF

NORCAP, (1998) *Searching for Family Connections*, London: NORCAP

Pugh, G (1999) *Unlocking the Past: The impact of access to Barnardo's childcare records,* Aldershot: Gower

Singer, D and Hunter, M, (eds) (2003) *Assisted Human Reproduction: Psychological and ethical dilemmas*, London and Philadelphia: WURRTriseliotis, J (1973) *In Search of Origins: The experience of adopted people*, London: Routledge, Kegan and Paul

Stafford, G (2001) *Where to Find Adoption Records*, London: BAAF

Treacher, A and Katz, I (eds) (2000) *The Dynamics of Adoption: Social and personal perspectives*, London: Jessica Kingsley Publishers

Wadia-Ellis, S (1996) *The Adoption Reader. Birth mothers, adoptive mothers and adopted daughters tell their stories*, London: The Women's Press

Useful addresses

USEFUL ADDRESSES

Adoption UK
Manor Farm, Appletree Road
Chipping Warden
Banbury
Oxfordshire OX17 1LH
Tel: 01327 260295

ADOPT – Northern Ireland
The Peskett Centre
2/2a Windsor Road
Lisburn Road
Belfast BT9 7FQ
Tel: 028 9038 2353

BAAF Adoption and Fostering
200 Union Street
London SE1 0LX
Tel: 020 7593 2000

The Children's Society
Edward Rudolf House
Margery Street
London WC1X 0JL
Tel: 0845 300 1128

The Children's Society
Post Adoption and Care:
    Counselling and Research Project
41 Queens Road
Peckham
London SE15 2EZ
Tel: 020 732 4089

Church of Ireland Adoption Society
Church of Ireland House
61–67 Donegall Street
Belfast BT1 2QH
Tel: 02890 233885

Family Care Birthlink
21 Castle Street
Edinburgh
EH2 3DN
Tel: 0131 225 6441

NCH
85 Highbury Park
London N5 1UD
Tel: 020 7704 7000

NORCAP
112 Church Road
Wheatley
Oxon OX33 1LU
Tel: 01865 875000

Parents for Children
41 Southgate Road
London N1 3JP
Tel: 020 7359 7530

Registrar General (England and Wales)
Adoptions Section
Smedley Hydro
Trafalgar Road
Southport
Merseyside PR8 2HH
Tel: 0151 471 4313

Registrar General (Northern Ireland)
Oxford House
49–55 Chichester Street
Belfast BT1 4HL
Tel: 02890 252000

Registrar General (Scotland)
New Register House
3 West Register Street
Edinburgh EH1 3YL
Tel: 0131 334 0380

→

Barnardo's

Barnardo's
Tanners Lane
Barkingside
Ilford
Essex IG6 1QG
Tel: 020 8550 8822

Barnardo's Cymru
11–15 Columbus Walk
Brigantine Place
Atlantic Wharf
Cardiff CF10 4BZ
Tel: 029 2049 3387

Barnardo's Northern Ireland
542–544 Upper Newtownards Road
Belfast BT4 3HE
Tel: 028 9067 2366

Barnardo's Scottish Adoption Advice
Service
16 Sandyford Place
Glasgow G3 7NB
Tel: 0141 339 0772

Post-adoption centres

After Adoption
12–14 Chapel Street
Salford
Manchester M3 7NN
Tel: 0161 839 4930

After Adoption Wales
7 Neville Street
Riverside
Cardiff CF11 6LP
Tel: 0800 0568578

After Adoption Yorkshire
31 Moor Road
Headingley
Leeds LS6 4BG
Tel: 0113 230 2100

Merseyside Adoption Centre
316–317 Coopers Building
Church Street
Liverpool L1 3AA
Tel: 0151 709 9122

Post Adoption Centre
5 Torriano Mews
Torriano Avenue
London NW5 2RZ
Tel: 020 7284 0555

West Midlands Post Adoption Service
4th Floor, Smithfield House
Digbeth
Birmingham B5 6BF
Tel: 0121 666 6014

Addresses of social services departments and social work departments can be found in the telephone directory under the name of the local authority.

Addresses of the Catholic Children's Societies are listed under individual diocesan entries in the *Catholic Directory* available in any public library or under the name of the diocese in the telephone directory.